Not Ours to See

A Memoir

Donna,

Walk by faith
and you will never
walk alone.

Anne Saunter Lieb

10/11/2023

Not Ours to See

A Memoir

ANNE SAUTER LIEB

with Beth Huffman

proving
press

Book Design & Production:
Columbus Publishing Lab
www.ColumbusPublishingLab.com

Paperback ISBN: 978-1-63337-672-4
E-Book ISBN: 978-1-63337-673-1

Printed in the United States of America
1 3 5 7 9 10 8 6 4 2

THIS BOOK IS DEDICATED TO MY DAUGHTERS.

Prologue

I stood at the stove with my back to Dad. As I flipped the over-easy egg in the skillet, the bacon grease splattered on my hand. I drew back and turned down the heat, while he continued talking about the past, as if I had never heard the same stories before.

"Annie, how are my granddaughters?"

"They're busy taking care of their families and working full-time. You'll get to see them at Thanksgiving. They love coming to the farm."

I poured a cup of coffee and sat across the table from this stubborn 86-year-old man who had mellowed very little with age.

"Annie, did I ever tell you that I spent 364 days in combat? Then I was put on a transport truck with other soldiers who fought on the front line. I was the last to be dropped off with my new orders. I found myself in front of a school in a small French village. That's when I met your mother who lived down the street. She was so beautiful. Marguerite and I were just getting to know each other when I received different orders and was sent to Germany. I wrote to her often and visited when I returned to the village. We married in the fall of 1945. After the war, I was offered a good job in Europe. I wanted to stay but there was pressure from my family to return home and help on the farm."

Mystery

After breakfast, he was ready to relax in his recliner. Within minutes, he fell asleep and didn't move when I tucked a blanket around his feeble frame that was covered with skin so thin it could tear. He was clearly exhausted from taking care of Mom. Not once did he ever complain.

I went upstairs to check on her. She was swollen from fluid retention and her breathing was labored. Poor health was destroying her body and spirit. The beige sweater clung to her puffed up arms. Her head rested on the pillow and I could see her gray roots, which was so uncharacteristic of this proud woman who had always maintained such a tidy appearance. At the age of 83, her fair complexion remained unblemished. When I laid my hand on her cheek, she looked at me with her radiant green eyes.

"How are you feeling, Mom?"

"Oh, Annie, I'm so tired and can't get warm. I put this sweater on but I'm still cold."

I grabbed the folded quilt, a gift they received on their 50th wedding anniversary, and wrapped it around her. I leaned over and said, "Is there anything special you'd like for me to do this afternoon?"

"There is something. I need you to go through the closet in the guest bedroom. It's a mess. Please sort through the sheets and towels and whatever is piled on top."

"Sure. I'll do it after I get you something to eat."

"No, I'm not hungry. I just want to rest. Your dad will bring me a sandwich later."

"Okay. I'll check on you in a little bit."

I walked across the hall to the room where I once slept. When I was a child, it had often been my refuge ... a place where I could temporarily escape Dad's wrath. Who was he really? I was told by my grandmother that he wrote beautiful letters to the family and Mom during the war. I had a hard time believing that. I couldn't get past the painful memories when he punished me as a child and controlled me unfairly as a teenager. All I ever wanted was his affection that I didn't receive. He made me feel like I didn't belong.

Questions

Dad startled me when his voice boomed from the bottom of the stairs, "Annie, what are you doing?"

"I'm cleaning out the closet for Mom. I'll be down soon. She'd like something for lunch."

"I'm fixing it right now. I just wondered what you were doing."

While he shuffled off to the kitchen, I finished organizing one of the shelves. When I walked into the bedroom to tell her what I'd gotten done, I heard the motorized chair creeping up the stairs.

"Mom, let me help you sit up. I'm making good progress but still have a little bit to do. I don't have time to finish it today."

She patted my hand and smiled.

As Dad set the tray on her lap, I reached over and kissed her forehead. "I have an appointment tomorrow but I'll see you next week."

"Annie, thanks for spending time with your mother and me."

"You're welcome. I'll check my calendar when I get home. I'll let you know what day I'm coming back."

I drove the familiar roads in silence. My head throbbed with questions that I was afraid to ask. What was the truth about my birth? Maybe I wasn't premature, even though I only weighed 4 pounds. I was born in late April but was always told that I was due in June. Was I conceived before they were married? If a young girl got pregnant in

Mom's culture, she would be married off to the first available man. No family was to be disgraced with an out-of-wedlock birth.

I couldn't imagine how much she struggled when she was pregnant with me. She was so young and in love with an American soldier who promised he'd come back for her. She had to feel alone and afraid. What if Dad didn't keep his promise? What if he was upset about the pregnancy? What if it happened at an inopportune time? Maybe that's why I felt like he resented me. Did he ever say he loved me in the letters he wrote to Mom? I knew where they were and I was determined to read them when the time was right. I needed to know the truth ... whatever that might be.

The Return

I couldn't control the tears driving home. Mom was gravely ill. Dad didn't realize it. He was so occupied in taking care of her that he thought she would cheat death and never leave him. I was still a mess when I got home. Before taking off my coat, I picked up the kitchen phone and called the agent about my upcoming trip to Ireland.

"Hello. I have a question. How long do I have before I can cancel and still get my money back? My mother is ill and I'm not sure if I should go."

I was relieved after our conversation and so glad that I bought travel insurance.

A few days later, my cell phone rang and when I saw the name on the screen, I braced myself for bad news.

"Dad, is something wrong?"

"Your mother fell. She tripped over a curb on the way into a restaurant. I told her to wait and let me help her but she didn't listen."

"Did she break anything?"

"No. She fell face-first and landed on her glasses. She has several cuts and bruises. She's in a lot of pain."

"I'll pack a bag and be there tomorrow."

She was lying on the living room couch when I arrived. Deep black bruises circled both of her eyes. She grimaced and said, "I look awful, don't I?"

"As hard as you fell, things could be so much worse, Mom. Did you lose your balance?"

"I have no idea what happened. My body hurts all over."

"Do you want help getting to the bathroom before I help Dad fix dinner?"

"Not yet. An ice bag would be good. I'm not sure if it's time for another pain pill."

She winced when we helped her sit up to eat. After a few bites, she wanted to lie back down. When I fluffed up her pillows, she said in a weak voice, "Goodnight, Annie."

"Goodnight. I'm going upstairs to read a little bit before bed. I hope you have a better day tomorrow, Mom."

Surprises

I came downstairs when I heard Dad making a pot of coffee in the kitchen. Mom was in a deep sleep, so I tiptoed through the living room.

I didn't want to startle him and quietly said, "Good morning. How did Mom get along?"

"She had a restless night. I was awake all hours, trying to make her comfortable. She's finally sleeping. Let's go out on the porch and talk."

As soon as we sat down, I could see the relief in his eyes when I said, "I'm going to be here for several days. I don't want to leave while she's in this much pain. The weather is supposed to be nice all week and I'm hoping she'll feel up to going for a ride."

"That would be good. I'd like to go with you."

"We'll make a point to do it. There's something else I want to talk about while we have this time together, Dad. I need your help with a project I've been working on for a few months. I'm trying to gather information on Mom's family history and yours. Once it's finished, I want each of my girls to have a copy. They often ask questions about their ancestors that I can't answer. I'd love to hear stories about you and Mom and our journey to America."

"There are so many that I'm not sure where to begin."

"Tell me about her family and what her life was like during the war. I know so little."

"Your mother's parents, Adrienne and Pierre, were hard workers. You already know that Marguerite has two younger sisters, Renee and Colette, and that Adrienne had 10 children in 20 years. Marguerite tended to many of the babies and even assisted at a few of the births. Five of them died from an unknown ailment, one from pneumonia and the other from meningitis. Their deaths were hard for your mother to accept. She blamed God for letting so many terrible things happen. She told Adrienne that she would never live her life like that and have so many babies die in her arms."

"Mom did tell me once that her father was very strict. In spite of that, she said that she knew he loved her."

"That's all true. He expected her to do chores and work long hours at the cafe. He was short-tempered with all of his daughters. His drinking got worse after his brother-in-law fired him from managing a lumber business. He was distraught over that, the war, and the deaths of his children. Demons ate away at him and he hit the bottle hard."

"Was anyone with Grandpa Pierre when he died?"

"Adrienne and your aunts were there. Your mother always regretted that she wasn't. She had been sent to her grandfather's farm to gather potatoes. She put herself in great danger running through the woods because the Germans could have captured her. There were gruesome stories of young women being raped, tortured and killed. She returned home safely but it was a few minutes after Pierre took his last breath. He was only 47."

"That had to be so hard on Mom."

"It was. She broke down when she saw his body. She kissed his cheek and laid a linen cover over his face. At that moment, she promised her mother that she would do whatever it took to help her family survive."

"I knew she went through a lot during the war but she's never gone into detail. I can't imagine how horrible it was for her."

"Your mother was strong like Adrienne. Several months after Pierre's death, the family faced a food crisis. Marguerite was 17 at the time and was considered an adult. Renee was 15 and Colette was only 3 years old. Each family received food rations based on their ages and job responsibilities. They pooled their food together but it wasn't enough to live on. Marguerite put herself in jeopardy frequently when she returned to her grandfather's farm."

"I don't know how Mom found the courage to do all that. She was too young to have so much responsibility."

"She had no other choice. It made her sick to her stomach when a German soldier came into the cafe one day and rubbed against her when he walked by. She wanted to spit on the filthy animal but she wasn't allowed to show her disgust. When some soldiers took over a room for their meetings, Adrienne reminded her that she had to do her job and be polite. She hated having to cook for them."

Just as I was starting to ask another question, Mom called out. She couldn't get up from the sofa on her own. As we helped her to the bathroom, she said, "I can't believe I slept that long. Charlie, what did the two of you talk about all that time?"

"You know me, Guite. I always have plenty of stories to tell."

Uncertain

Once Mom's pain subsided and she regained some strength, we took a drive through the country on a sunny day. Dad stayed home to visit with a neighbor who stopped by. Even though she knew I was hoping to learn more about my ancestry, it was very difficult for her to open up.

"Mom, tell me more about your life during the war. Didn't you resent having to work such long days at the cafe? What would you rather have been doing?"

"I didn't resent it because that's probably what kept us alive. In the back of my mind, I wanted to go to college but I knew that would never happen. I was very good with numbers and wanted to study mathematics. We didn't have much money and I couldn't leave the cafe. That was hard to accept because my life had been so different when I was a young girl. We lived in a beautiful chateau but had to move when Papa lost his job. We had no other choice."

"Dad's eyes lit up when he described seeing you for the first time. Did you feel the same way about him? Was it love at first sight for you too?"

"He was very polite but I wasn't attracted to him at first. He was too skinny. Maman called him the little American. When he asked me to go to a dance, things changed. We had a wonderful time. One thing led to another, I guess. When we started taking long walks, we became more than friends and he asked for my hand in marriage. Things like that happened very quickly during the war. When we got married, we had only known each other four months. Even though he promised Maman that he would give me a wonderful life in America, I had misgivings about leaving my family. I was afraid what would happen to them."

"I don't know how you survived emotionally when you were pregnant and Dad was so far away."

"I had no other choice but to get through it. I had heard many disturbing stories about young girls who went overseas with GIs. Many of them returned home ... alone and heartbroken. I didn't want to be one of them. I ate very little because rations were low and my stomach was constantly tied in knots. When Maman and other relatives eventually learned I was pregnant, they were so excited and fussed all over me. I was afraid I wouldn't be a good mother."

"Was I born at home?"

"That was my plan until my friends insisted on making an appointment with a midwife. They were worried because I didn't gain much weight. It was a pretty day on April 30th when I went for the examination. I was nervous when I had to undress and put on a robe. When the midwife moved her hand across my belly, she didn't think your head was in the right position. She put her hand inside me and tried to move you into place. I screamed in pain. She told me you would be born soon. She also said that she would have never examined me like that if she knew how far along I was."

"Was the midwife right? Was I born soon?"

"You certainly were! My water broke when I started walking back to the cafe. I somehow made it home. When Maman saw how pale I was, I told her what the midwife said. There was so much pressure when I went to the bathroom that I could feel you coming. Maman immediately got in touch with our family friend, Henri, who had a car. We barely made it to the hospital in time. You were born in the hallway and came out bottom first. You were so tiny. We were in the hospital for two weeks. Maman wired Charlie about your birth and he came as soon as he could. You were such a happy baby. Maman, Aunt Renee and Aunt Colette helped me take care of you for the first two years of your life. I don't know what I would have done without them. Do you have fond memories of them or were you too young to remember?"

"I remember a lot. I'll never forget the sounds of their laughter. They were so sad the day we left for America. I cried when they waved goodbye. My life was never the same after that, Mom."

"Neither was mine, Annie. Neither was mine."

August 1947

My arms were wrapped tightly around Papa's neck when we boarded the train. I stared at the man in the dark uniform who tipped his hat and smiled.

"Charlie, give Annie to me. I do not want her sitting on these cushions. They are too scratchy. I'm holding her until we get to Paris."

"It's going to take six hours to get there. When she falls asleep, you can lay her down."

"No. I will hold her. She feels safe in my arms."

"Guite, I know you're nervous but everything will be fine."

"I am not sure of that."

"I've promised you a good life and I will give you that. When we get to Paris, I'll need to pick up some important paperwork. From there, we'll get on a train to Le Havre. That's where we'll board the ship. Does it make you feel better to know what's going to happen?"

"No, it doesn't. All of this is going to be so hard on Annie. I've told you many times that she is too young for a big trip like this. You have not been there much of her life. That is why you do not understand. I will not talk about this anymore."

"It's important for you to listen to me, Guite. When we get off the train, you'll carry Annie and I'll grab the luggage. We have to walk quickly to get a good place in line. There will be a huge crowd of people. They'll

15

be pushing and bumping into each other. Stay right behind me."

When I started to get fussy, Maman rocked me back and forth and sang a familiar lullaby. Her voice lulled me to sleep until the train came to a screeching stop. She whispered, "I have you, little one. Don't be afraid."

"Guite, hurry up. She'll be fine."

But I wasn't fine and I cried when Maman had to walk so fast that she had trouble holding me. She kept yelling, "Too fast, Charlie! Too fast!"

"Keep moving. We can't stop now. I can see the end of the line."

"No! You must slow down. I almost dropped Annie!"

He finally turned around and waited.

"Take some deep breaths, while I get in line."

"I'm tired, Charlie. I feel sick. It's dirty here. People smell like urine and alcohol."

"Lower your voice. You have to be careful what you say. The good news is that the line is moving. It won't take long for me to get a taxi when it's our turn. The three of us will sit in the back. Don't say anything about the driver when we get in. He'll honk his horn constantly and he'll drive very fast. When we reach the hotel, I'll get the luggage and pay him. Wait for me in the lobby."

Maman's body never stopped shaking until the driver hit the brakes. He sounded mad when he yelled, "This is where you get out. Hurry up! I don't have all day!"

It was so noisy outside that I started crying. Maman did her best to calm me down.

"Oh, this building is tall, Annie. It touches the sky. And look at the glass door. It goes round and round. Let's walk through it and wait for Papa."

Maman hadn't smiled once during our trip but that changed when we walked into a room with a bed. She put me down on the soft carpet where I could crawl.

"Here we are, Guite. I told you we would have a nice room. Do you like it?"

"It's very nice, Charlie. The three of us will fit in the bed."

"I'll be gone when you wake up tomorrow. I'm picking up the paper-work at the United States Lines office. We'll go for breakfast when I get back."

Papa wasn't happy when he returned. Maman and I were looking out the window at the Eiffel Tower when he said, "I'm afraid I have dis-appointing news. It looks like we'll be spending a week in Paris. We won't board the ship until August 1st now. It will take 12 days to get to America. I'm upset about the delay but there's nothing we can do about it. We have to wait. I'm as surprised as you are."

"I'm not surprised. Your letters had promises of when you'd visit me. I waited and waited and you didn't come."

"You know that wasn't my fault, Guite. When you're in the military, you have to follow their orders. There are many wonderful things to see in Paris. We'll stay busy and the time will pass quickly. I already have a surprise for you tonight."

"Thank you. Where are you taking us?"

"We're going to a nice restaurant and after that, we'll see a show."

"Annie can't sit still that long. She's too young."

"I know she is. That's why I hired one of the hotel's babysitters to watch her."

"Charlie, this can't be! I will not leave her. I don't know this person."

"People hire babysitters all the time in America. Besides, it's too late to cancel."

"I'm not going."

"Yes, you are. I already bought the tickets. The babysitter will be here soon."

"Do not make demands, Charlie."

When there was a knock at the door, I quickly crawled to Maman. Papa invited the person in.

"Thank you for coming. Our daughter will cry after we leave but then she'll settle down."

He walked over to Maman who was holding me tight.

"Let go of her, Guite. She'll be fine."

"Charlie, your loud voice is upsetting her even more. I will hand her to the person."

Before she did, she whispered in my ear, "I will be back soon. I promise."

When she walked out the door, I curled up on the floor and wailed, "Maman! Maman!"

Accident

I pointed at the object in the water that got bigger and bigger. Papa started talking quickly to Maman who was carrying me.

"Guite, the walkway to the ship will be shaky. Don't look down at the swirling water. It will scare you. When we get to the top of the ramp, the men and women might get separated. I've heard of that happening. Don't worry. I will still find a way to see you and Annie."

"Where will they take us? I don't want to be alone without you."

"You'll have a small room. There might be a porthole where you can look outside. You will probably have to share a bunk with another woman."

"Come find us as soon as you can."

Maman waved goodbye to Papa and carried me into the room. She was happy when a lady offered to hold her small luggage bag.

"Thank you. I have been carrying my little one for days. My back aches."

"You're welcome to sit on the bottom bunk and rest. I'll move my things out of the way."

"You are very kind. I need to unpack first."

"I can hold your daughter while you do that."

"Thank you but she'll cry. Our long trip has been hard on her. She is very tired. Do you mind if my husband visits us?"

"Not at all. Let me at least help you unpack."

Maman held me on her lap while she talked to the nice lady. They were interrupted when Papa knocked on the door. I crawled to him and giggled when he held me up in the air.

"Charlie, this is my roommate. We enjoy each other very much. Let me have Annie. We are using the top bunk and I need to lay her down for a nap. She can't keep her eyes open."

Maman waited until my eyes were closed and when she thought I was asleep, she turned around to hug Papa. Seconds later, there was a terrifying thud when I rolled off the bed.

"My God, Guite! Her head hit the cement floor! I'm running her to the hospital ward. I'm not sure if she's breathing!"

When the doctor laid me on the table, Maman was hysterical and kept saying, "She can't die! Is she breathing? Save our baby!"

He looked at Papa and said, "I need for you both to step back while I examine her."

Maman never stopped crying until he said, "She's pale and listless but her heartbeat is strong. She hit her head so hard that she was knocked unconscious. Her moaning sounds are a good sign. That means she's waking up. Babies are resilient. She wasn't seriously hurt. She's lucky to be alive."

Drastic

After many restless nights of being separated, it was rewarding for Maman and Papa to be together and experience the dramatic skyline of the New York Harbor and Statue of Liberty. I was fascinated by all of the bright lights.

"Guite, there is going to be another big crowd when we get off the ship. I'll need to go to the GI section and you'll have to undergo a physical examination. You'll need to show your documentation. We need to be patient with the process. Keep telling yourself that the last stretch of the journey is almost over."

"I won't complain. I was worried Annie might get sick on the trip but she didn't. I'm thankful."

"I'm looking forward to showing you my family's land. I know this will be a drastic change in lifestyle for you. Even though you're a city girl, I think you'll adapt to country living. It's probably going to take some time for me to get used to things again too. I've been away for nearly six years. I was in my third year of college when I joined the military and now I'm a husband and a father. I'm a battlefield survivor who took care of concentration camp refugees after the war. I've changed."

When the train started to pull into the station, Papa put me on his lap.

"Guite, I can see my parents and sister standing on the platform. They're waving at us. They can't wait to meet you and Annie."

Maman braced herself when she saw them running towards us. I was scared and buried my face in her chest. They cried when they hugged Papa.

"Son, you look tired."

"We all are, Mother. It was a long trip."

When we got in the car, it was so crowded that I started to whimper. While Papa described the things he wanted Maman to see, she was feeling my cheeks and forehead. The closer we got to the big yellow house, the worse my stomach felt from the heat and cigar smoke. The unfamiliar smells of the cows, pigs and horses made things worse. When I started getting sick, Maman yelled to stop the car quickly.

As soon as we walked in the house, she handed me to Papa and said, "I need to use the lavatory. It has been a long time."

"Follow me, Guite."

He opened the door to a room filled with supplies and kitchen equipment. There were magazines piled in neat stacks, laundry tubs, clothes and shoes for every season. Chamber pots were lined up in a row.

"Charlie, is this where I go?"

"No, you'll go outside. Those are for the nighttime."

She was uneasy when we walked down a path that led to several small yellow buildings. I covered my nose and Maman gasped for air when she opened one of the doors. She looked at Papa in disbelief.

"I don't go in there, do I?"

"Yes. I'll shut the door for you. You'll get used to it."

Alone

Maman was so happy when she saw where we'd sleep. She couldn't stop talking about it.

"Charlie, it was nice of your parents to give up their larger bedroom for us and bring in a baby bed. I appreciate what they've done. Please hand me the fresh linens. I want to make our bed."

"You can do it later. I want to show you the farm and maybe stop by to see some friends. Annie can stay here."

"She is so tired after all the traveling. So am I. Can we please stay home?"

"No. I've already talked to my father about driving his car. Get Annie. We're leaving."

"Charlie, she doesn't know them. She'll be afraid. Give her time. Besides, you told me your parents would love her but they've shown no signs of affection. Your mother was stern when she told me that she wants to be called Meme or Grandmother. Your father is to be called Grandpa."

He didn't pay attention to anything she said and picked me up.

"Guite, let's go."

When we got to the bottom of the stairs, he put me on the second step. The two people stood on the landing. Papa looked at them and said, "Thanks for watching her. She'll stop crying. We won't be gone long. I put a gallon of gas in the tank."

He walked out the front door and pulled Maman behind him when the man said, "Son, that won't be enough gas. That car eats it up. Stay here."

I tried to slip between the two people but they wouldn't move. They ignored me when I reached out and screamed "Maman!" again and again. When I was finally worn out from crying, they walked away in silence. I was afraid of them, so I stayed on the step and scratched the bottoms of my feet that itched from the coarse wool carpet. I buried my face in my white cotton nightshirt that Aunt Renee embroidered with the letter A. I closed my eyes and pretended that Maman was rocking me to sleep.

The Rules

As the months passed, I started talking in short sentences and walking on my own. I was more comfortable around my grandparents and grew accustomed to Meme's structured routines. On Monday, the house was filled with the clean fragrance of laundry that was hung outside to dry. Clothing was ironed on Tuesday and mended on Wednesday. She meticulously cleaned the house on Thursday, shopped on Friday and spent Saturday preparing food for Sunday's dinner.

She took a break each day at precisely 4 o'clock and enjoyed a cup of tea in the parlor. I was never allowed in, unless it was Saturday night when the entire family gathered there. The house resonated with beautiful music when Meme played the piano, accompanied by Papa on the violin, my aunt on the trumpet and Grandpa on the trombone or drums. Once the evening was over, it was bedtime because everyone was expected to be in church the next morning. That was Meme's rule.

On mending day, she spent hours in her bedroom, working away on the old treadle sewing machine. I was allowed to watch if I was quiet. One day, I paid close attention when she said, "Annie, did you notice what I did with each straight pin after I was finished? While the fabric moved along, I placed it in the red pin cushion. You must always put the needles away. Watch where they are at all times. Never place them on your lips. If one goes in your body, it will go to your heart and you will die."

When Maman tucked me in that night, she said, "Did you have fun watching Meme sew today?"

"No. I'm afraid of the needles."

"Why?"

"She said if one goes in my body, I'll die."

"Meme didn't mean to scare you. She was just warning you to be careful."

After I got past that scare, Meme took me with her to the hen house. She made it very clear what was expected of me.

"You can help me collect eggs from the chickens' nests. Watch your step and be quiet. We must not scare the chickens or they will not lay their eggs. Some could break if the chickens fly around."

We entered on tiptoes, listening to the hens cackle as we approached the nesting area. I held my breath and watched Meme gently slide her hand into the straw. She pulled out an egg and carefully put it in the wire basket. Then she nodded that it was my turn. I was tentative at first but I liked the tickling sensation and the feel of the warm egg. Unfortunately, it was too large for my small hand and I dropped it. When I yelled out in disappointment, the hens flew everywhere. Meme was so mad.

"The hens will not lay. We must leave now or more eggs will break! I need those for the egg man."

She grabbed my arm and quickly led me back to the farmhouse. Even though I told her I was sorry, she said, "I told you to be quiet, Annie! You won't be going back again."

Some mornings, I peeked into the back room and watched Papa and Grandpa take their shaving mugs down from the shelf. They whisked their brushes until white foam rose to the top. After they smeared it all over their faces, Grandpa reached for the leather strap that he used to polish his razor. Then he carefully scraped away the suds. I was afraid of the leather strap, especially if it was in Papa's hands.

Confrontation

It wasn't unusual for Papa to work in the fields all day with Grandpa. I was glad when he was outside because when he was in the house, no one seemed to do anything right. He was angry about something or mad at someone all the time. My aunt took me to the store one day and bought me a wallet. When we returned home, I excitedly held it up and said, "Look, Papa!"

His face turned red when he looked at her and yelled, "Why did you buy that? I don't want her to be spoiled!"

They argued for a long time but in the end, I had to give it back. I decided then that I would never ask for anything again.

At dinnertime, we ate at a large, round table that was perfectly set with a tablecloth, silverware, napkins and a centerpiece of fresh flowers. Meme always wanted the meal to be prepared on time, so she asked Grandpa each morning when he expected the day's work to be done. I dreaded dinner because I feared what might happen, especially if Papa was in a bad mood. After Grandpa prayed, Mama would often lean over and whisper, "Please, Charlie, no problems tonight."

Her pleas to protect me rarely helped. He typically glared at me from across the table, pointed his finger and said, "You have to eat. If you don't, I will punish you with the leather strap and you will be sent to bed. I don't want another night like last night."

When I stared at my food, he slammed the utensils on his plate and shouted, "How can you not eat? I watched children starve during the war. They looked through garbage cans and picked up food left behind by the rats! How can you sit there?"

I had no trouble watching Meme prepare the food but I gagged at the thought of eating it. I wanted to throw up when the mashed potatoes, dripping with chicken gravy, got close to my mouth. I couldn't help it. Nothing tasted like the food I used to eat. When I continued to stare at my plate, he roared, "Eat now!"

Everyone watched as he stood, pushed his chair away from the table and walked towards me. He put me under his arm in a tight grip, headed to the back room and grabbed the strap. He didn't stop whipping me until my cries turned into screams.

When the weather was nice, Mama took me outside where we sat on the large stone stoop. She did everything she could to help me eat and avoid Papa's temper.

"I want you to open your mouth when I bring the spoon to your lips, Annie. Please do it for me." Even though I didn't want to upset her, my lips remained sealed.

One night, Papa put a clock in front of me at the table. He pointed to a number and said, "If you have not finished your food by the time the hand reaches the six, you will be switched and sent to bed."

I stared at it, while Mama and the others looked away. They wanted him to stop punishing me but he wouldn't listen. They were afraid to say anything in fear he'd hurt me more. When the time was up, he went outside and returned with a tree branch. He stood in front of me and slowly peeled off the leaves and twigs.

"If you don't eat, I will use this on your bare legs. Do you hear me?"

Minutes later, the branch nubs burned welts into my skin. The more I screamed, the harder he lashed out. When he put me in bed, I was crying so hard that I struggled to catch my breath. He didn't feel sorry for me at all and walked away. When he returned to the table, he spoke in a threatening way.

"I don't want to hear a word from anyone. I know how to handle this. She is not going to be an ungrateful child and she will NOT control me! I will break her. I will! I trained many soldiers and she is no different."

Meme looked up from her plate and said, "Charles, I don't know who you are now. Since coming back from the war, you are not the same person. Please call the doctor and let him examine Annie."

When he started mumbling to himself, Mama stood and started to walk away.

"Do not comfort her, Guite. I forbid it."

"I'm going upstairs to my room. I don't need your permission to do that. What Meme said is true. You are not the same person."

Several days later, we were in the doctor's office. During the exam, he noticed the red marks on my legs. He looked directly at Papa and said, "She is small for her size but healthy. Her eyes are alert and there is a good texture to her hair. She is doing well and she will eat when she is ready. Let me say that again. She will eat when she is ready."

Papa didn't like his answer.

"Doc, while children are starving in Europe, she doesn't eat the food placed in front of her. Something must be wrong. She's strong-willed and I will break her of that."

"This has nothing to do with the starving children in Europe or being strong-willed. She isn't the first child I've seen who doesn't want to eat what's on her plate. She'll eat enough to survive during the day. Let her be. She'll eat when the time is right."

As we left the office, Papa reached for my hand but I pulled away and ran to Mama. He muttered, "What does the doctor know? He wasn't over there, Guite. He didn't see people starving."

"The doctor knows best, Charlie. Not you."

Although he continued to berate me at mealtime, the whippings stopped. When I still wouldn't eat, he took me to the kitchen and put the plate of food in front of me. I wasn't allowed to get up until he gave me permission. As soon as he left, I stared at the counter where Meme always set the freshly baked cinnamon rolls that she made from leftover pie crust. Once everyone had finished eating, I was excused. I purposely didn't leave the kitchen until Papa and Grandpa went outside to do the chores. When Mama and Meme were busy doing the dishes, I reached up for one small cinnamon roll that fit perfectly in my hand. I slipped out undetected and escaped to my favorite getaway … the enclosed front porch with the white wicker swing.

I never got caught, even though I was pretty sure that Mama and Meme saw me.

Lonely

Mama often felt so alone in the house because she had little interaction with anyone. When Papa wasn't helping with farm work, he was attending college classes and it wasn't unusual for Meme and my aunt to spend hours on sewing projects upstairs. Mama finally told Papa when she'd had enough.

"Annie and I need to be with you, Charlie. I want us to spend time together as a family. This place isn't our home. I waited for you after the war and now we must be together. I can't take this any longer."

"I understand what you're saying. My folks wanted us to stay with them when we returned. It was a good way to get adjusted to this lifestyle again but I know it's time to be on our own. Please be patient a little bit longer. I'll figure something out, Guite."

In the summer, Mama and I sat in the watermelon patch and ate the fruit that Grandpa planted. One afternoon, I noticed that her belly was much rounder.

"Mama, did you eat too many seeds?"

"No," she laughed. "You will have a baby brother or sister soon."

A few months later, my sister was born. Mama put her in my crib and moved me to the room across the hall. Bedtime suddenly became scary when I watched large shadows play on the wall. I knew I couldn't cry or Papa would spank me. The only time I felt safe was when I snuggled under the blanket and sucked my thumb. He was so upset with me and said more than once, "If you suck your thumb, it will fall off. Stop it now or your teeth will be crooked. If you don't listen to me, I'm going to rub something smelly all over it."

None of his threats fazed me. I didn't stop until Mama said other kids would make fun of me.

Even though I did my best not to anger Papa, my curiosity got me in trouble more than once. One Sunday afternoon, I picked up a small container of liquid on Mama's bedroom dresser. After I drank some of it, I dropped the glass and cried out, "Bad taste!" When Mama saw what I'd done, she screamed, "She drank kerosene! We must get her to the doctor!"

After he gave me something that made me vomit, he assured Mama that I would start feeling better right away. Papa showed no compassion. He looked at Mama and said, "She won't eat her dinner but she drinks kerosene. What's wrong with her?"

New Start

Mama's smile turned into giddy laughter when she swung me around and said, "We're moving to the big city with Papa!" Even though I wasn't sure what that meant, it had to be good news because I'd never seen her so excited.

I soon realized that the big city meant Columbus where he would finish his education. Because he went to school during the day and worked at night, Mama didn't see much of him. She was alone with my sister and me most of the time. She didn't mind, though, because she was happy in our small apartment with a tiny kitchen, living room, bathroom and bedroom. She enjoyed becoming friends with other housewives in the "village" which was GI housing that resembled barracks. She especially looked forward to Friday nights when they visited friends who lived above us. The women talked, the kids played in a corner of the room, and the men stared at a small circle in a box called a television.

The large field behind the barracks was an ideal playground. Even though I was 5 years old, I had never played with other kids prior to the move. I quickly learned how to play hide-and-seek and to chew certain leaves that tasted like bursts of spearmint. Whenever Papa saw me heading outside, he said, "Don't go close to those large rocks. Stay in the field to play."

During a game of follow-the-leader one afternoon, I wandered out by the road with all the others and climbed the rocks. Even though I knew

I'd get in trouble if he saw me, I gave in to the dares when my friends said, "Don't be a scaredy-cat. Jump on them. It's fun."

On my first attempt, I lost my balance and fell. The jagged rock ripped a chunk of skin just below my knee. When I screamed in pain, two of my friends ran back to the barracks to get Mama. They were surprised when Papa opened the door instead.

Once he realized that I didn't have a head injury, he scolded me in front of everyone and shouted, "I told you not to go near the rocks. See what happens when you don't listen!" He embarrassed me further when he threw me over his shoulder and paddled me, while blood streamed down my leg. My friends couldn't believe how mad he was and ran home as fast as they could.

Mama gasped at the sight of the open gash and followed us into the bathroom where he plopped me on the toilet seat. I screamed when I saw the bottle of alcohol in his hand.

"No alcohol, Papa! Please don't use alcohol. I won't climb the rocks again! I'm sorry!"

I got light-headed and nearly passed out from the searing pain. Mama held me until he barked out the order, "Get the medical student upstairs." I begged her not to go, petrified that he would use more alcohol.

"Mama, stay with me. I'm afraid."

Papa didn't give her a chance to answer.

"I don't care if you are afraid. Maybe that's a good thing. Maybe you'll start listening now."

Mama kissed my cheek and said, "It's okay. I'll be right back."

A few minutes later, the student arrived with his medical bag. He stretched adhesive tape tightly across it and said, "The cut is deep. You'll have a scar on your leg. You'll have to stay off of it for several days until it begins to heal."

Papa's temper was still on fire.

"I told you to stay away from the rocks. This is your own fault. So quit crying NOW!"

I sometimes wondered if he would ever stop getting so mad at me. One day, we visited friends in another neighborhood and I accidentally left my doll in the car. When I realized it, I asked him to get it for me. He was busy talking and said, "I'll get it later. Don't interrupt."

When he and the other men went into the house, I decided to get it myself. I looked both ways before crossing the street but didn't realize my little sister was not far behind. I saw her in time to grab her dress by the collar and pull her back, just before the oncoming car stopped. The brakes screeched and the driver sped off. When she landed on her bottom and started to cry, everyone came out. After I explained what happened, Mama's friend said, "You saved your sister's life."

Papa didn't see it that way. He picked me up, put me under his arm and paddled me.

"Didn't I tell you to wait? Why can't you listen?"

Small Town

I put my books and dolls in the box and pushed it towards the others that were stacked along the wall. While I watched Papa hitch the small green trailer to the back of the car, I kept thinking about the conversation I overheard earlier in the week.

"Guite, now that I've finished my education, we'll be leaving Columbus as soon as possible. I'm looking forward to teaching in a small town. I know you loved living in the city but you'll get used to this change. It will just take some time. That's all."

She didn't answer him, knowing he'd already made up his mind. When she told me about it, I said, "I'll never get to see my friends again. Neither will you, Mama."

"We'll visit Suzy. Papa likes the family. Always remember that we'll take a lot of good memories with us, Annie. The good news is that he found a house. He said we'll like it. You'll be able to make new friends. The move won't be easy but it's something we must do. A wife goes where her husband's job takes him. He's the one who makes the money that puts food on the table."

A few days later, I looked out the car window and waved goodbye to all of my friends. When they disappeared from view, I slid down in the seat. I wondered if he meant it when he said to Mama's friends, "I'll bring Marguerite back to visit. We'll stay in touch."

The two-hour drive felt like five and he was the only one in good spirits.

"We're here, girls. This is the town. This is where we're going to live."

My sister looked up from Mama's lap and I stared at a horse hitched to a post. Some of the old buildings were ready to collapse. Things got prettier when we turned down a side street. I loved the large trees. When we stopped in front of a red brick house, my eyes got big. I waved at the two girls across the street who were playing hopscotch. My heart started racing when they waved back. When we walked through the house, Mama said, "This rental is too small for our family, Charlie. It only has one bedroom and there is another family living on the second floor. We'll have to look for a larger place."

"I've already put money down, Guite. We need to unpack and settle in, so that I can get off to a good start with my classes. We'll talk about a bigger rental when the time is right."

A week later, it was time for school to start. When Mama tucked me in, she said, "I can't believe you're in 1st grade already."

"I know. I'll learn how to read and write. Some of the kids might be smarter than me if they went to kindergarten. Why wouldn't Papa let me go when we lived in Columbus?"

"He thought it was a waste of time and too far away. But I know you'll work very hard and get good grades."

All of my excitement turned to dread when he took me to school the next day. I didn't want to walk down the steps to the dark basement. I was shaking when I met my teacher who was an older lady. Instead of telling me to have a good day, Papa walked away and said, "Pay attention."

The school was so damp and cold in the winter that I got sick easily and had to stay home many days. I was already behind in my reading assignments and my absences made things worse. It was humiliating when I mispronounced words and the kids snickered. As a result, I became shy and withdrawn. I didn't enjoy anything except coloring and art projects.

When Papa left the house in the evenings for meetings, he always said, "Guite, you have to work with her. She's way behind. Use the flash-cards. Don't give in if she says she's tired. Make her do them."

No matter how long we worked, I couldn't remember the words. In exasperation, I often laid my head on the table and cried.

"Mama, I'm trying but I never get them right. It's embarrassing when I make a mistake. I want to be in the blue bird group with the smart kids. I don't like being in the yellow one. Everybody knows it's the lowest one. Our teacher puts us at desks away from the rest of the class and gives us extra help. I feel sick to my stomach sometimes. I want to learn but I don't know how. You believe me, don't you?"

"I do. We'll keep working. Maybe you'll become friends with some of the children in your reading group. Then you won't feel so different. Who sits across from you?"

"A boy named Earl. He's always smiling and laughs a lot. He can't sit still. The teacher told him to be quiet the other day but he didn't listen. So she grabbed him by the back of his shirt and bent him over the desk. Mrs. Smith spanked him so hard with a long wooden paddle that my desk started moving. He cried for a long time. I'm always going to be good in school because I don't want that to happen to me."

At dinner that night, I never looked up from my plate. I was afraid to make eye contact with Papa who was raging mad after a bad experience with a realtor earlier that day.

"Guite, I can't believe he took us to look at those houses. The one place smelled and we could hardly walk through the other ones because of all the empty containers."

"You didn't need to get so angry and yell at him, Charlie. He's doing his best to help us find a bigger place."

"His best isn't good enough. I'm glad I gave him a piece of my mind. Those houses were an insult to my integrity and upbringing. I was respected as a soldier and I expect to be treated with respect as a civilian.

Besides, a student of mine told me after class that his father has a rental. He's willing to lower the rate since I'm his son's teacher. We'll go through it this weekend."

Main Street

Even though the house we moved into was 150 years old, I liked it. The huge backyard had an outbuilding so large that it looked like a small barn. I converted it into the perfect playhouse. Mama, who was expecting another baby, appreciated all of the additional space and the lush vegetable garden. There were two bedrooms upstairs and mine was the coldest. When the single-pane windows frosted over each winter, I slept in two pair of pajamas, hats, gloves, socks and six layers of blankets.

Summertime with my friends on Main Street was pure fun. We played at the park, had bike races and captured lightning bugs in Mason jars. Because we didn't live far from downtown, I often walked to the five-and-ten-cent store and stared at the penny candy, paper dolls and coloring books. Even though I never had any money, I liked to look until the lady behind the counter routinely said, "You need to move on. If you aren't here to shop, you need to leave. Come back with your mother."

I was miserable whenever it rained and I had to stay inside. Mama always said, "Pick up a book and read. Keep busy."

I did what I was told but the same thing always happened. I stared at the page and couldn't concentrate. Reading the same sentences twice didn't help. Oddly enough, I liked going to the library and checking out several books at a time. Inevitably, they wouldn't get read and I'd forget to return them.

"Annie, these overdue notices are unnecessary. Why can't you remember to take them back on time?"

"I'm sorry, Mama. I don't know why I forget."

"Papa wants me to teach you some French but I'm not going to do it. It's too frustrating when I help you with homework and you don't focus."

"Maybe you can teach me some words when I'm older. Maybe I'll be able to remember things better then. I bet you miss speaking French to your family."

"I do miss it but I'm here now."

"Why don't you go back and see everyone?"

"It costs too much. I'll go back one day but not now. Who would take care of you if I went away?"

"It makes me sad to think about that. I don't want you to ever leave."

The Visitor

Even though she was often exhausted taking care of my baby brother and looking after my sister and me, Mama was always very gracious when someone stopped by. When this happened, I knew what was expected of me. I had to go upstairs and make very little noise. When the choir director from our church stopped by one evening, I made the mistake of not obeying. Instead of going to my room, I started dancing and showing off to get his attention.

Papa smiled and said, "Annie, please settle down. Go upstairs. We're talking."

After ignoring him, he asked again but I still didn't listen. The second our guest left, he yelled, "Annie, come here!"

As I tentatively approached him, he grabbed my arm forcefully and turned me over his knee. I had been paddled by him many times but never that hard. Mama ran into the room when I screamed, "Papa, you're hurting me!"

She shrieked, "Charlie, that's enough! You've gone too far!"

I ran to my room and heard him shout, "I will NEVER be embarrassed by her like that again, Guite!"

Mama had learned through the years that it was impossible to reason with him when he was that angry. He had threatened to break my spirit many times and he finally succeeded. It broke her heart to watch me withdraw from conversations, especially when he was nearby. I became so timid that I never spoke to an adult, unless they initiated a conversation. Even then, I only said a few words.

One night, Mama checked on me after I said my prayers. When she sat on the edge of the bed, I said, "I have a favorite picture on the wall at Sunday school. Jesus is smiling at the children. They're sitting at his feet. Papa never smiles at me like that. He likes my brother and sister more. Do you think he loves me?"

"He loves you, Annie. He just doesn't know how to show it."

Absent

My inability to concentrate in elementary school was very evident midway through 1st grade. It didn't help that I was absent for 37 days, due to one cold after another. Unless I was doing an art project, I stared out the window. I wasn't being defiant when I daydreamed. For whatever reason, I couldn't help it. Being reprimanded by my teacher didn't change anything. I really wasn't surprised when she wrote these comments on my report card:

Annie hasn't made the improvement in reading that I had hoped for. I feel this is due to her sickness. If she will go over the little reading cards and especially the phrase cards regularly for a couple of weeks, it should help.

I knew that I had to show it to Mama and Papa and decided that the dinner table would be the best place. The problem was that I didn't have a chance. No one was ever allowed to interrupt Papa who dominated the entire conversation with stories about the war and his students. It wasn't until bedtime that I had Mama's full attention. I pulled it out from underneath my pillow and said, "My teacher said to show you this."

After reading it, she said, "I don't understand. I know you're a good girl in school but you have to get better grades. I'll help you as much as I can with the reading cards but I'm so busy getting dinner ready and taking care of your brother that you'll have to practice on your own sometimes. Do you understand?"

"Yes. I'll try harder."

As soon as she went downstairs, I heard her say, "Charlie, please put down your school papers. You need to read what Annie's teacher wrote on her report card. It will do no good to get mad because she's trying."

He scanned it quickly and said, "She'll never get accepted to Ohio State with low grades. I don't have time to help her. She needs to learn self-discipline. That's the only way she'll succeed."

"She's only in 1st grade. You can't expect her to be self-disciplined. She's such a bright little girl. I hope her teachers can figure out why reading comprehension is so hard for her. Otherwise, the struggle will follow her through grade school."

My attitude improved in second grade when we moved to a new school building. The overall learning atmosphere was better. Plus, I loved my teacher and was motivated by her encouraging words. I had mostly B's and a C in spelling. I thought Papa would praise me but instead he said that he was disappointed I didn't get straight A's. Third grade was much like 2nd had been. Once again, I loved my teacher and responded well to her teaching approach. Fourth grade, however, was a different story. My teacher petrified me and I ended up missing 16 days because of the mumps. She sent a note home to my parents that read:

What can we do to get her to speed up in arithmetic? I give her homework but she seldom turns it in.

Fifth grade was a terrible experience and my grades showed it. Instead of having four subjects, I was expected to learn seven of them. Just thinking about it made me nervous. I always did much better on tests with multiple choice answers but that changed when I was required to write sentences and paragraphs. It took me forever to unravel my thoughts. I spent more time staring at the blank page. My teacher was sweet but she had very little class control and the noisy environment made it even harder to think.

My sixth-grade year found me preparing for confirmation. I put off completing the packet of questions that the minister gave me. It was too overwhelming. As a result, I wasn't prepared when he gave me the oral exam. When he realized that I couldn't retain all of the information, he said, "Annie, I'm only going to give you one question on Sunday when you sit in front of the congregation. Memorize the answer. Can you do that? I don't want this to upset you."

"Yes, I can do it. Thank you."

Even though Mama seldom went to church with us, she was there for my confirmation. When we got home that afternoon, I said, "Why do you get to stay at home on Sundays and I have to go to church?"

She looked at me with an expression that meant not to bring it up again and said, "Because your brother cries and I don't want him to be a distraction."

We visited our grandparents often. They seldom came to see us because Grandpa had too many chores. I adored the quiet, soft-spoken man who taught me how to play the flute. I often wondered why Papa couldn't have been more like him. Meme tried to teach me how to play the piano, but I could never get my left hand to cooperate and she eventually gave up.

One summer, I got to spend a week at the farm by myself. If I wasn't coloring or doing paint-by-number kits, I went outside and drew pictures. Grandpa surprised me one afternoon and said, "Annie, come into the parlor. I have something for you." I gave him a huge hug when I saw the oil painting kit and the canvas he'd set up on the card table. When I told Meme how excited I was, I said, "May I have a piece of fancy paper to write to Mama and Papa? I want to tell them how much fun I'm having."

She went to her desk and pulled out an envelope and a sheet of stationery that was embossed with tiny flowers. I spent so much time using my best penmanship because I wanted them to be proud of me. When I returned home and they didn't mention it, I brought it up at dinner.

"Mama, I hope you and Papa got my surprise in the mail."

He looked at me and said, "That was the worst letter I've ever read. You don't know how to write. What have you learned in school? Everything was wrong. You should be ashamed."

He got up and walked away to grade papers. It felt like his students mattered more to him than I did. I was so hurt that I never wrote them another letter again.

Different

By the time I was ready to start 6th grade, my classmates were keenly aware of my learning issues. They witnessed it multiple times when my teachers reprimanded me. One particular day was especially humiliating. During a math lesson, the teacher put a problem on the blackboard that she wanted someone to solve. I was staring out the window when she sarcastically said, "Annie, since you seem so interested, please come forward and answer it."

I stuttered, "I-I don't know how to do it."

When some of my classmates erupted in laughter, she made no effort to curb it. I hung my head until the bell rang. Mama was in the kitchen making vegetable soup when I got home.

She asked how my day had gone and when I didn't answer, she saw my tears.

"Annie, let's sit at the table. Scoot your chair beside mine and tell me what's wrong."

"I don't want to go back to school."

"But I thought you liked it."

"I do but it's too hard. I try to keep up but I can't. My mind goes blank. I'm different from the other kids. They're smarter than me."

"I'll let Papa know. It might help if he talks to your teacher."

"That will make things worse. He won't listen to her advice anyhow.

He's never listened to any of my teachers. He'll just get mad and yell at me to try harder. Something is wrong with me."

"Maybe you'll have a better day tomorrow. Just do your best. Besides, I will have a big surprise for you when you get home."

"Tell me. Please don't make me wait."

"Your Aunt Colette and her husband, Lef, are coming to visit."

The Reunion

I was so excited that it was impossible to sleep. I loved Aunt Colette. She and Aunt Renee spoiled me so much when I was little. Even though Mama was terribly homesick to see them, she never complained. After we moved to the States, she kept in touch with everyone through letters. Papa told her it would cost $50 to make a call overseas and she knew they could never afford that. Many years later, she was delighted when the cost dropped to $1.70 for every three minutes, if calls were made at night. At the end of each conversation, they were all in tears when it was time to say goodbye.

I got up extra early the next morning and stared at the clock, waiting for them to arrive. When they were over an hour late, Mama was afraid they were lost and told Papa that we needed to get in the car and find them. When we started driving down the street, I noticed a fancy car I'd never seen before and said, "That's them! Turn around!" Papa honked and after he got their attention, he motioned for them to follow us. Mama and Aunt Colette couldn't stop smiling and waving at each other. When we got to the house, they started crying and hugging each other in the driveway. Finally, Papa said, "Let's go inside. Guite has prepared a lot of food."

When they started talking fast in French, Lef chuckled and said, "Ladies, we have no idea what you're saying." Aunt Colette apologized and said to me fondly, "My sweet Annie, I rocked you to sleep when you were a baby and look at you now. You're such a pretty girl."

After we were seated at the dinner table, Mama said, "Please tell us everything about you and the family." Lef smiled and said, "Marguerite, once she starts talking, she'll never stop."

As it turned out, he was right. She had so many stories to tell and I was mesmerized by them all. She took a sip of water and said, "When Mother remarried in 1948, it was hard for me to accept. I was only 11 years old and wasn't going to take advice from her husband. I resented how domineering and jealous he was. He demanded all of her attention. He didn't like her being friendly with the customers at the cafe and talked her into selling it five years later. We then moved to a very small house when I was 16. I didn't like it because my bedroom on the second floor was very cold. I was also lonely because Renee was married. I couldn't wait to get away, so I moved into a one-room apartment in Nancy and started working in a canning factory. I enjoyed working with the machinery. When I was 17, I met Lef at a party. He was a soldier from New Jersey. We quickly fell in love and were married in France."

After Mama tucked me in that night, I knew she was anxious to join her sister in the living room where they could be alone. Once I heard them talking, I slipped out of bed and sat at the top of the stairs to hear more.

"Colette, you were so much younger when I worked at the cafe during the war. Mother always told me that I had to be polite to everyone, including the German soldiers. I knew I had to be careful what I said. I must not have been careful enough, though, because a customer left me a note. He warned me that I needed to stop complaining about the Germans because someone could hear me and turn me in. Looking back, I took too many chances. I hid a radio under my bed and listened to a station out of Beirut, Lebanon. The Germans would have shot me if they knew what I was doing. Papa could have gotten in a lot of trouble too. He had strong political views and when you're in business, you can't discuss politics. After he got fired at his job, he was on his own and started drinking too much. Some days, Mother had to get him out of bed. Thank God he bought the cafe for security."

Colette sighed and said, "I was only two when he died. I don't remember him much. I've always felt bad about that."

"You were also too young to remember how hard it was to find food. We had a garden and kept rabbits behind the cafe. When we didn't have leftovers from meals we cooked for the Germans, we survived on pigeons, horse meat, frog legs, and food from the black market. I'll never forget when Charlie came into the cafe with the container of Spam that he gave to Mother. It was an apology for yelling at you when you stole the wood from their storeroom. That Spam was the best thing we tasted in a long time. I still enjoy a can of it today."

"I don't know why I disobeyed Mother and ran away sometimes, Marguerite. Maybe I was just trying to get attention. I'm sure I didn't understand that I could be caught by the Germans. I do remember collecting cigarette butts, drying them out and re-rolling them to sell. I also picked violets, put them in a bunch and sold them. I was always trying to think of ways to make a few cents."

Then Mama lowered her voice to a whisper and said, "I've never told anyone about the day I went alone to confession. I was only 12. One of the staff members got fresh with me and I couldn't get away fast enough."

I tiptoed back to bed. Now I knew why Mama didn't go to church.

Changes

One week before 7th grade started, Mama said, "Annie, we need to go into town to buy you some bras. Be ready in a few minutes. Papa will be home to watch the kids while we're gone."

I raced up the stairs to change from my t-shirt to a blouse. I was anxious to get some, hoping they would help me look more like the girls in my class who had wider hips, long hair and full breasts. Compared to them, I looked like a little girl. While I was getting ready, I could hear Papa's reaction when Mama told him where we were going.

He laughed sarcastically.

"Guite, why are you buying those for her? She has nothing to put in a bra. What a waste of money."

"No, she needs the training bra. It's what the girls are wearing. It's time, Charlie. She'll have a gym class this year and she can't wear t-shirts. We'll be back soon."

Just once, it would have been nice to receive a compliment or a gesture of support from him. I was so thankful for Mama.

Because the two elementary schools combined for our 7th grade year, we had to return to the large dungeon, the red brick building I hated in 1st grade. That alone was depressing but what made things worse is that we were put in classes based on our abilities. I found myself in a class with the bright kids who got good grades. I knew I didn't belong there. I had a feeling that Papa talked to the counselors and pressured them to make the decision. He was a proud man and worried what people would think of him if his daughter wasn't in the smart class. I never felt like I was better than anyone else in school but he felt like our family was better than most. Image was very important to him, even if it was at my expense sometimes.

I was lost and totally unequipped for such a drastic change. I didn't get anything out of the first few days. As I stared out the window, my mind wandered more than ever. If that weren't enough, my struggles went beyond the classroom walls. We had lockers with combination locks. I fumbled with mine several times and decided it was easier to carry all my books that weighed more than I did. I finally took the combination lock home and made a game of it until I figured out the process. It was a small victory that would have been laughable to my classmates.

I listened to the teachers rattle on about things I didn't understand. They could probably tell from my blank expressions. I didn't see the point in conjugating verbs and I really didn't care if participles dangled or not. On the first day of geography class, the teacher handed me a gigantic book. It was so heavy that I accidentally dropped it on my desk. It landed with a loud thump. I knew then that I was doomed and my below average grades proved it. I hated the fact that Papa knew what was going on in all of my classes. He often embarrassed me in front of everyone at dinner when he typically said, "So I heard you had trouble in some of your classes today. You did poorly on the tests. Tell me why."

I knew why but I couldn't tell him that. We were forbidden to talk back. He would have gone on a tirade about being disrespectful. I wanted to say, "I'm in the wrong class. You know it's true but you won't admit it."

I hated the monotony of reading and answering worksheets. I needed assignments that allowed me to use my hands and be creative. I was finally given that chance in the spring when my science teacher required us to create a nutrition notebook. After he explained what he wanted and showed us an example, I understood what I had to do. I poured all my energy into it and received an A on the project and a B in the class. I couldn't wait to run home and tell Mama.

Awakening

I was actually looking forward to 8th grade because it meant being on the east side of the high school building which was much nicer. I was excited about playing my flute with the older band students, even though I knew I'd feel inferior in their presence. I yearned to look like the popular girls who wore blouses, shorter skirts and bobby socks with saddle shoes.

Early in the school year, I wanted to attend the fall festival with my friends. I was hopeful Dad would let me go because he was going to be there to supervise a booth that he and his students set up. My hands were dripping with sweat when I said, "May I go?"

"No. It's just a place to spend money."

"But Sue and Barb are going. Please."

He and Mom debated the issue in French until he finally said, "I guess you can go but I'll drop you off and will bring you back home. Understood?"

"Yes. Thank you."

I was nervous the entire night and kept looking over my shoulder to be sure that he wasn't watching my every move. After I visited the booths and competed for some prizes, my body started itching all over. Dad took me home immediately when I told him what was happening. Mom was devastated when she saw me. I could hardly breathe and my face, eyelids and fingers were swollen beyond recognition. She laid wet towels on my face and arms while Dad called the doctor who came right away. He gave me a shot and I soon fell asleep. When Mom asked him what caused the swelling, he said that I was allergic to something but he didn't know what. It was gone the next day but I was exhausted.

Even though I wanted to meet guys, it was unnerving when one started calling and wouldn't identify himself. I thought it was someone in the senior class because he and his friend always watched me. Whenever we made eye contact, I felt self-conscious and looked away. I knew, of course, that I wasn't allowed to date an upperclassman but I did feel special. Dad's desk was right beside the telephone stand and whenever someone called me, he would immediately pounce and say, "Who is that? Hang up. I don't want boys calling this house. You are too young."

We had several school dances that year that I wasn't allowed to attend. I got tired of hearing him say, "You'll have more dances during high school. You don't have to go now." He thought I wanted to go just to be with guys. I would have liked that but they weren't interested in me. I wanted to go because I loved dancing with my friends. I decided not to argue about going to some of them because the one I really wanted to attend was in the spring. When that time came, I took a risk and brought it up when we were having dinner with my grandparents.

"Dad, there's a dance next week and I'm going."

He stood up and yelled, "You are doing what? You don't tell me you are going to the dance. You ask me! You are not going. I know what's best for you."

As I stared at the floor and said nothing, my throat began to itch and my eyes started to swell. I had another attack but this time there was no Benadryl to help, so Grandmother held compresses on my forehead until the swelling subsided.

One week later, he gave me permission to go. That could only mean one thing. Mom had defended me again. As it turned out, I didn't enjoy the evening because I felt guilty for putting her in that position.

I had looked so forward to the dance at the end of the year. Another verbal battle ensued between Mom and Dad before he relented and said I could go. She was more open to new ideas when she became involved with other mothers through school activities. She wanted me to be like the other girls and thought I should have a new dress. Even though I never got to pick out my clothes and didn't have many, I appreciated what I had. There were times when I came home from school and something new would be hanging in my closet. Every dress she bought fit me perfectly.

The summer before my freshman year, our 8th grade band had the opportunity to join the high school band for concerts in the park. One evening, a cute guy from the junior class walked me home. As we got closer to the house, I said, "You can't walk me to the porch. My dad will be mad if he sees us together. It's nothing against you but I'm not supposed to be with boys."

Unfortunately, Dad had already spotted us and when I walked in, he exploded. "You are not to walk home with an upperclassman! You walk home with the girls only."

One night when I couldn't sleep, I overheard Mom talking to him in the kitchen.

"Charlie, you need to spend time with Annie. You will never know who she is before she leaves home. You need to do something positive with her, instead of reprimanding her so much."

The next week, he invited me to join his class on a trip to the Enrico Fermi power plant in Michigan. I didn't mind being the only girl with 25 boys but I was too shy to talk to them. I was glad that I went but it wasn't exactly what I thought spending personal time with Dad meant. That all changed one summer afternoon when we were at the farm and he said, "I'll teach you how to drive. Let's go down the back roads."

I caught on fast. He told me to pay attention to my driving but never yelled at me once. Instead, he started talking about the war.

"You know, when I was in Europe, I worked nearly 20 hours a day, seven days a week. We all worked hard then. People don't know how to work today. I carried a 22 Beretta on my shoulder and a knife in my belt. I had to kill a lot of enemy soldiers. It was either kill or be killed. A lot of my buddies died. I held some of them in my arms and saw them take their last breath. I'll never forget that look in their eyes and my uniform covered with their blood. No one can understand what war does to you unless you've lived it. The sound of gunfire and crawling over mutilated body parts never leaves you. There is no escaping the smell of death. I had a hard time adjusting to things when I returned home."

I was unsure if I should say anything. It seemed like he was in a trance. I was relieved when he finally said, "We should head home now, Annie. Your mother will wonder where we are."

Drills

I grabbed a piece of toast on my way to the first practice with the high school band. My classmates and I wanted to make a good impression with the director and got there early. The smug upperclassmen soon pulled up in their shiny cars and ignored us. The drum major headed to the field immediately and I watched in awe as he threw the baton high in the air and caught it each time.

When the director called us onto the field, a skinny guy pulled up in a two-tone green 1956 Ford. The director spoke into the megaphone and said, "Bob, you're a line captain and you need to be here on time."

"Sorry, I had car trouble," the cocky kid replied, while nonchalantly holding a clarinet upright in his hand. He didn't pay attention to anyone else when he walked towards the drum major. After they laughed about something, he walked over to his line.

The director pulled a pile of papers from a box and passed out stapled packets. As I ruffled through the sheets of directions, it all looked like a bunch of x's which I quickly learned were the diagrams that had to be memorized. After receiving music to clip on our instruments, I listened carefully to his speech.

"Each mistake you make equals one demerit. An accumulation of demerits reduces your grade. Now look at your assignment sheet and get in formation. Freshmen, go to the sidelines and watch the show we performed last year. After that, go home and study. Come back prepared tomorrow morning."

I walked off the field and wondered if I'd be able to memorize it all. That was going to be the tricky part. On top of that, I couldn't get the skinny kid out of my mind, especially when he smiled at me.

After two weeks of intense practices in the humid August heat, we were all glad when it was over. When we were putting our instruments away on the last day, my friend, Pat, couldn't wait to share some good news.

"Annie, I've seen Bob looking at you. He's my brother's best friend. He works a lot of hours at a grocery store and still manages to get straight A's. He's planning on going to college. I hope you're ready for this because he wants to talk to you in the band room Monday morning."

I was nervous all weekend. I had rarely talked to any boy, let alone an upperclassman. Dad knew the names of every troublemaker in school and Bob's name never came up, so I was hopeful he was one of the good guys. After our classroom practice ended, I was cleaning my flute in front of the storage area and acted surprised when I heard his voice.

"Hi Annie."

"Hi."

"I hope you're doing well and learning the ropes."

"I am."

"I'd like to walk you to your next class. May I?"

Although I told him that he could, I was petrified that Dad would see me in the hall with him.

"Listen, the Homecoming dance is coming up. I'd like to take you."

I knew I was blushing when I said, "Thank you. I'll have to ask my father. I'll let you know. Bye."

That night, I anxiously waited for Dad to finish talking at the dinner table. When he paused to take a drink, I said, "Please excuse me but I'd like to ask a question. I met this guy in band. His name is Bob and he asked me to the Homecoming dance. May I go?"

Without considering it at all, he said, "I don't think so. It's for upperclassmen."

"But a lot of girls in my class are going."

Mom put her hand on his arm and said, "Charlie, it's only a dance and they have chaperones."

He stared at me with his piercing blue eyes and said, "Yes, I guess you can go but only to the dance and then you have to come straight home. You will not date until you are 16. Be sure your friend knows this is not a date. Do you understand?"

"Yes, I do. Thank you for letting me go."

I spent hours getting ready and making sure my shoulder length hair looked perfect. I felt grown up in my red wool sheath dress and black heels that matched the skinny black leather belt that hung loosely at my waist. When I walked into the dining room, I was taken aback because Dad actually smiled and said, "Marguerite, I think we have a young lady in the house. You sure look lovely, Annie."

When Bob and I left the house, Dad still had to have the final word and said in a semi-threatening tone, "Remember your curfew."

We had such a good time. I loved being in his arms. As soon as the dance was over, he took me straight home. When we pulled into the driveway and he reached over to kiss me, I wasn't sure which way to move my head. Before our lips touched, he leaned back when he noticed the shade going down at our neighbor's house. I laughed and said, "Oh, don't worry about that. She does it all the time when she sees lights in the driveway."

As we stood on the porch holding hands, I said, "Bob, thank you for a wonderful evening."

"You're welcome. I had a nice time too."

We continued to talk in school as often as possible. I wondered if he'd ask me to be his date for the winter dance. When he did, I ran it by

Mom first. She must have told Dad right away because he gave me permission before I even asked. It was a wonderful night that only got better when Bob took off his class ring and put it in my hand.

"Annie, will you be my girl?"

"Yes! But you know I can't date until I'm 16. I can't let Dad see your ring. I'll hide it under some clothes in my dresser."

Unforeseen

As his Junior Prom approached, we both avoided talking about the fact that I was an underclassman and wasn't allowed to go as his date. I was the one who finally brought it up.

"Bob, you should go. It isn't fair for you to miss it because of me. I really want you to invite someone."

He thought about it and said, "Who should I ask?"

After I mentioned a couple of girls who weren't dating anybody, he asked one of them a few days later and she accepted. The night of prom, I was a server at the punch table. It was impossible not to be jealous when he held the girl in his arms the same way he held me. Even though I had no one to blame but myself, I resented their having so much fun together. I considered telling him how much it bothered me but decided against it because I knew I was being immature.

Shortly before turning 16, Dad grilled me repeatedly about getting my driver's license.

"Listen to me, Annie. You can't be too careful when you start driving. It's better to go places in the car alone, instead of having friends with you. They'll be talking and laughing and you could easily be distracted."

He also made a point to tell me about the high school girls who got pregnant. Each time he lectured me about appropriate behavior, I was tempted to say, "I will never get in trouble and I will never get pregnant before I'm married. You don't have to worry."

A few days before my birthday, Bob asked if my parents were going to have a party for me. After I explained that they didn't believe in things like that, he insisted on having one with his parents. When he picked me up that night, Mom and Dad said very little about my spending time with his family. They were still unhappy about the onyx necklace he bought me for Christmas. As soon as we got in the car, he gave me my present. Inside the narrow box was a watch that fit my small wrist perfectly.

"Bob, I'm speechless. It's beautiful. I've never received such a lavish gift."

I was smiling when I got home and set the cake box on the table. Mom and Dad were still up. I said, "Help yourself. Bob's mother bought it for me. It's delicious."

Mom shook her head and said, "They shouldn't have done such a thing. That's too much."

I quickly dialed down my upbeat tone and said, "I don't understand. What is wrong with a cake? And what is wrong with this watch Bob gave me?"

Dad shouted, "You have to give it back immediately!"

"But it's a gift."

"What are his intentions? What does he expect from you?"

"Nothing. He expects nothing from me, Dad. He's very respectful. We enjoy being together and I'm not giving it back."

I turned and walked upstairs while they exchanged heated words in French. A week later, I announced that he and I were going steady.

"You are what?" Dad yelled. "You will only go out once a month and you will be home by 11 o'clock. That's final."

I wore his class ring on a chain around my neck and once a week, we wore matching shirts. I was flattered that someone so smart was interested in me. I meant it when I told Dad that he didn't expect anything from me.

He was always a gentleman and simply gave me a kiss at the end of the evening. He had a promising future and wanted to be successful in life. Why couldn't my parents see that?

In the spring of his senior year, we faced the same dilemma with prom as the previous year. I wasn't old enough to be his date. When he asked me who to invite, I gave him the names of three girls who I didn't think he'd find attractive. The thought of him dancing with someone else again was unbearable.

The week after prom, he avoided me at school. I had no idea why, so I was glad when he finally called and wanted to come over. I knew something was wrong when he didn't make eye contact. I was expecting him to say that he didn't have a good time and that he thought about me the entire night. Instead, he mumbled that he really liked the girl and wanted to date her. When I realized he meant it, I felt like such a fool.

Several days later, I was half-heartedly doing my homework when the phone rang. I grabbed the receiver before anyone else ran into the room.

"Hey, it's Bob."

"Yes."

"Annie, I'm sorry. I made a mistake breaking up with you. Can we start again?"

I should have told him how hurt I was but I didn't. I should have held him accountable and asked why he changed his mind suddenly but I didn't do that either. I jumped right back into the relationship.

Things with Bob continued to go well until my friend, Carolyn, invited us to a party at her house one Friday night. As I watched him interact with others and ignore me completely, I had enough. He'd done it one too many times. When I told him we needed to talk, we walked over to a corner of the room.

"I'm breaking up with you. You're distant with me and I don't deserve to be treated like this."

I was melancholy the next morning and when Mom sensed I was

upset, she tried to lift my spirits.

"Annie, do you want to go to town with us?"

"No, I have work to do."

After they left, I debated if I should call him. Even though what I'd said to him was true, I regretted breaking things off. My hand shook when I dialed his number.

"Hello."

"Yes, it's Annie. We need to talk. Can you come over?"

"I'll be right there."

I nervously stood in the driveway waiting for him. When he got out of the car, I couldn't hug him soon enough.

"Bob, I'm sorry. I overreacted. I don't want to break up. You'll be leaving for college soon and I don't want anything to hurt our relationship."

Busy

I was miserable when he left for an out-of-state university. He rarely came home and I knew my parents would never allow me to go see him on a weekend. In spite of the obstacles, I thought we'd be in touch frequently but that didn't happen. He wrote very few letters and never called. When I questioned him, the response was always the same. He said that his classes were demanding and that he was too busy.

I needed distractions to keep me from thinking about him constantly and made a point to get involved with club activities and planning for prom. My parents and I traveled to several cities before we found the perfect gown for my tiny figure. It was pale blue with a white ruffled back skirt. Bob was mesmerized when he saw me and made me feel like a princess on the dance floor.

During the summer, I went with my sister, grandmother and aunt on a train trip to visit relatives in Minnesota. They were refined people who made me realize what a simple and sheltered life I'd lived. I always felt inferior around them and envied my cousin, who spoke several languages and played the violin in an orchestra. Even though their lifestyle was impressive, I wouldn't have been comfortable living in that world. When I shared this with Bob one weekend, he showed little interest in anything I said. His attitude bothered me but I kept it to myself. He had such a hold on me that I avoided making him mad at all costs. Deep down, I worried that I wasn't good enough for him.

On a hot August day in 1963, I was wrapped up in watching television until Dad flipped the channel. I knew better than to say anything. We watched what my parents watched, whether we liked it or not. I normally didn't pay much attention to the news but that night, I was intrigued. I listened to a black man, Martin Luther King, Jr., who was speaking to an estimated crowd of 200,000 people who gathered around the Lincoln Memorial. I was captivated by his powerful presence when he described his dreams for his children and our nation. The only black person I knew was our custodian and his skin was so light that no one thought he was different from the rest of us. When Mom walked into the room, Dad said, "They are demanding equal rights."

I was far too naive to comprehend what that meant.

Chaos

When my classmates and I learned that the administration canceled our senior trip to New York in the spring, we were furious. Dad was one of the faculty members who made the decision. I wasted no time in expressing how unfair it was and how hard we all worked to afford it. I was disappointed but not surprised by his blunt response.

"Someone in last year's group caused a problem. Your class won't be going because we can't trust some of your classmates."

He didn't look at me when I reminded him how many hours I babysat and cooked at a local restaurant to pay my own way. The more I complained, the angrier he got for challenging him. I finally gave up when he dismissed my feelings completely.

Even though I had A's in band, the best decision I ever made was to drop it and take Home Economics classes. I was following the college preparatory schedule of classes with a major in Vocational Education. I loved the hands-on projects and our creative teacher who made class fun. As a member of the Future Teachers of America, one of my responsibilities was to record the attendance information for her each day. It occurred to me how quickly the school year was passing when I wrote: November 22, 1963. After returning to my sewing machine, I looked at the clock. It was 1:40 which meant the bell would ring shortly. I still had time to get more done. I placed the zipper placket under the zipper foot and began to sew when the PA system started to crackle. The principal cleared his throat twice and in a quivering voice said, "We just learned that President Kennedy has been shot while riding in a motorcade in Dallas, Texas. Students, I want you to go straight home when you are dismissed from class."

There was a long hush before our teacher said, "Please put your things away."

The hallway was quiet. Some students were crying as we exited the building. Many of us walked with our heads down, uncertain how this would affect our lives. When I met up with my friend, Sue, we hugged and cried together. She and her family were Irish Catholic and were big supporters of the President. Although he hadn't been my family's choice, I was sad too. How could we live in a world where this kind of violence existed?

When I got home, Mom was watching the tragedy on TV. I didn't know what to say because I had seldom seen her cry. She turned from the couch and said, "Annie, you're home early."

"We were dismissed because of what happened."

I sat down beside her and reached for a tissue when the cameras showed Mrs. Kennedy holding her dying husband in her arms. That Friday night, we all picked at our TV dinners and watched more unbelievable events unfold.

Chaos and tragedy ensued for months but our country slowly began to heal and we moved on with our lives. As winter was winding down, I stood outside the guidance counselor's office, waiting for my senior appointment. Having been accepted at OSU, I was anxious to discuss plans for the fall. When my name was called, he said, "Nice to see you. Please take a seat." Then he sat back in his chair and said, "Annie, are you ready for next year?"

"Yes, I am."

He opened my folder and glanced through the papers. He paused before saying, "You really aren't college material and will have a tough time in school. You have poor study skills."

I never heard another thing he said. When he finished, he asked if I had any questions.

"No. Thank you."

I turned and walked out. I was so disheartened that I didn't think to ask him why he thought I would have problems. I didn't tell my parents what he said or Dad would have been in his office the next morning.

I never made the honor roll. I was always a fraction of a point away but I was in the top quarter of my class. While I flourished in classes like typing, art, mechanical drawing and Home Economics, my grades in lecture classes barely improved, even when I forced myself to concentrate and take a lot of notes. When the counselor mentioned my weak study skills, I should have said, "I know that. Why didn't the school provide me with more help?"

Doubts

My two brothers shared a small bedroom and when I heard Mom say that she wished they weren't so cramped for space, I suggested buying bunk beds. She wanted no part of it, emphasizing how dangerous they could be.

"Annie, I never told you this but you fell from a bunk bed and landed on your head when we were on the ship. A doctor examined you right away and said you were fine but I made up my mind that you would never sleep on one again. You could have had a head injury. Thank God you didn't."

The more I thought about it, I couldn't help but wonder if I had a serious injury that went undetected. Maybe that's why I couldn't concentrate and struggled to learn. Maybe it wasn't my fault all those years when Dad yelled at me for not trying.

When I brought home the first paycheck from my new job at the turnpike plaza, it wasn't what they had promised and Dad was irate. Minutes later, we were in the car. I was on edge when he shook hands with my boss who had no idea what was coming.

"My daughter might as well stay home. This paycheck is ridiculous! She works awful hours and does not get paid what you promised her."

Once he was done ranting, my boss agreed to an increase. The next morning when Dad picked me up from work, he was still angry and didn't speak to me. I knew I had disappointed him when I didn't stick up for myself. But how could I when I'd always been told to respect my elders? I didn't know how to defend myself because I was afraid of the consequences. After I changed clothes, I glanced at the mail and opened a letter addressed to me.

September 1964
Dear Annie,

Hi! I am a sophomore at Ohio State this fall and will be your student advisor. With the beginning of classes only two weeks away, you are probably excited and maybe a little nervous. It is my pleasure to extend one of your first personal welcomes. You have a unique and rewarding experience ahead of you. I hope that your freshman year is as meaningful for you as mine was for me.

As I read the letter, I heard echoes of my guidance counselor saying, "You are not college material." What if he was right and I failed? With each passing day, I became less enthused about going but knew I couldn't admit it, especially to Dad. When the dreaded day finally arrived and we pulled up to my dormitory, they helped me unload everything. I was surrounded by ecstatic students who were tearfully hugging their families goodbye. Their demonstrations of affection were foreign to me. Mom gave me a quick hug and Dad said, "Stay on task. Don't fall behind."

I was actually relieved that they didn't stay long. I was worn out from Dad's lecture during the drive. I pretended like I was listening when he said, "You must get off to a good start with your classes. Your mother and I expect you to get good grades. We are paying a lot of money for you to attend college. We know you're happy that Bob transferred to Ohio State last year but you are too young to be serious about a guy. Your education MUST come first! Do not waste your valuable time being with him when you should be studying."

What my parents didn't know was that Bob and I had already made plans to meet on the Oval near Mirror Lake. It was my first Friday night on campus and I wanted to spend it with him. I was waiting outside when he walked up the sidewalk. I couldn't fall into his arms quickly enough and shivered as we kissed like two people who had been apart too long. We walked a short distance and found a park bench under a tree. He put his arm around me and said, "Annie, will you marry me when we graduate? I'll finish the same year that you do. What do you say?"

As surprised as I was, I didn't hesitate.

"Yes, I'll marry you! That will be a perfect time."

When I got back to the dorm, one of my friends noticed the joy I couldn't conceal.

"Hey, Annie, you seem happier than usual."

"I am! I love being with Bob."

I wanted to share the news but knew I had to keep it a secret. I couldn't risk my parents hearing about the proposal. They made it clear many times that I shouldn't be seeing an older guy and that I couldn't consider marrying anyone until I graduated.

After three weeks of classes, my school work became an unbearable chore. I was falling behind in everything and was ashamed of my grades. When my English professor called me in for a conference and explained what I needed to do on the next assignment, I had no idea what he meant. I didn't know how to function on my own and was afraid to ask anyone for help.

When I had a surprisingly good day at school, I called Bob to share the details. I knew we couldn't talk long because he reminded me twice that he was short on time. When I told him that I was eating dinner in the dorm with a wonderful group of friends I'd met, he asked me if any guys were there. When I said there were a few, he told me that I couldn't spend time with them or any other guys. Even though I resented his jealousy, I felt guilty for upsetting him and started sitting with a group of girls. What bothered me was how easily he put his feelings ahead of mine. I couldn't help but wonder if there were other things I didn't know about him.

I found it easier to study at the library. The dorm was too noisy. When I started taking notes one night, my throat began to itch and my skin started to tingle. I quickly gathered my things when I started breaking out in hives. When I felt my face swelling, I covered it up with my scarf and hurried to the elevator. My eyelids were barely open as I ran to the student health center.

One of the doctors said, "Please take this Benadryl and go back to the dorm. You'll need to rest."

My roommate was so startled by my appearance that she dropped her book. She did what she could and helped me into bed. The medicine knocked me out right away. I ended up missing another OSU game and fell behind even more with my studies.

By spring, I felt like I was getting my act together. I began to understand the process of college life and wasn't as intimidated. I thought about changing my Vocational Home Economics Education major to archaeology or history but Dad wouldn't let me. He insisted those majors were a waste of money and not suitable for a female.

As I began meeting new people, I gradually gained more self-confidence. I volunteered to help create costumes for the play *She Stoops to Conquer* and enjoyed participating in the drama department, which was one of my requirements. When my ability to focus improved, I started to become more aware of what it took to be successful. I even envisioned my graduation day. But all of the positivity I was feeling ended one spring afternoon when the phone rang. One of the girls said, "Annie, the call is for you. It's your mother."

I was thrilled because I had so much to tell her.

"Hello, Mom, it's so good to hear from you. How is everyone doing?"

"We are fine. How are your classes going? You know the family has made many sacrifices to send you to college. We have given up so much. You must do well."

After I said I understood, she talked about my siblings and what she and Dad couldn't afford to do for them because I was in school. When I hung up, I slid to the floor and prayed. *Lord, why am I causing so much distress for my family? Help me find an answer. I can't deprive them of what they need.*

My grades improved but it was going to take a long time to boost my grade point average, after making a mess of things in the fall quarter. I heard many students say that summer school classes were less stressful. If I was going to stay in college, I wanted to give it a try. On the other hand, I didn't want to be a burden to my family.

A few days later, Dad called. As usual, he did all the talking.

"Annie, our neighbor and friend, Mr. Buyer, has a job for you at the bank. You can have it if you stay at home and don't go back to college in the fall. Your grades have been poor, so don't plan on returning because you aren't. You will be trained in all aspects of banking. It's truly an opportunity of a lifetime. Do you understand what I'm saying?"

"Let me think about it."

"No, you need to come home Memorial Day weekend. I've already scheduled your interview. Thinking about it isn't an option."

"But that's a busy weekend with finals all next week, Dad."

"How many times do I have to tell you how important it is to come home? I told Mr. Buyer you're interested. There isn't anything else to say. Goodbye."

I was the obedient daughter and went to the interview. They wanted to hire me for the summer and longer.

Turmoil

Dad paced and fired one directive after another when I returned from the interview. I wasn't excited about the job and my silence indicated it.

"You will not join Bob in Columbus. That is out of the question. Mr. Buyer has offered you a job at the bank. The decision is made. Do you hear me? Don't look away when I'm speaking to you!"

I paused, knowing he wouldn't like what I was going to say.

"If you won't let me return to OSU, I want to enroll at the Columbus Business University. It has an excellent reputation and I'll have enough money saved from working at the bank to pay my own way when the winter quarter starts in January."

He looked at me with disgust, picked up the newspaper and slammed it on the coffee table as he left the room. On his way out, he said, "Marguerite, I'm going to school. I have work to do."

Mom looked aggravated and said, "See what you've done, Annie. He's going back to school instead of staying home with the family. You upset him again."

I sat down on the sofa and tried to digest what had just happened. My brothers, who were playing with a farm set, stared at me like I was a stranger. I was no longer comfortable in my own home but I had nowhere else to go. What hurt even more was knowing that Mom and I would no longer be as close. I had lost my best friend and advocate.

I enjoyed the employees at the bank. They patiently guided me through the training period that went well. When I got home from work one afternoon, I glanced at the mail and pulled out a letter addressed to me. I was surprised to see the name in the return address. It was from the boy who I always had a secret crush on in school. He was popular with the other girls and never looked my way. I lost track of him after he enlisted in the Navy right out of high school. I hurried to my room to read it.

July 27, 1965
Dear Annie,

I bet you are shocked to hear from me. I hope you're doing well. Are you going to college? It feels strange being out of school for a year. In some ways, I feel like I'm getting old. This world can change a person.

When I was in school, I couldn't wait to get out and now I'm taking USAFI courses. We just came back from Cannes, France. It is a beautiful place and country. Today is our second day in Genoa. I got my first test back today and was shocked when I scored an 82. That isn't too bad for a kid who dropped Algebra I the second day of high school.

Well, write and tell me what you're doing. I would very much like to have a picture of you. We should be in Philadelphia Yards in November. I plan to come home on weekends and would like to know if I may have the honor of taking you out.

John

I read the letter several times and couldn't put it down. If only he had asked me out earlier. I slowly stood up and reached for some stationery. I knew I couldn't put this off or I would give in. How did I write a Dear John letter when deep in my heart, I wanted to go out with him?

Dear John,

It was so lovely to hear from you. Yes, I spent one year at OSU. I won't go back in the fall because I'm planning to attend a business school in January. I will work at the bank until I enroll.

I'm happy to hear that all is going well with you. Enjoy your travels. Thank you for the invitation but I am going with someone and will be engaged soon.

Sincerely,

Annie

On the Tuesday before Thanksgiving, we were swamped at work with extra customers who were preparing for the holiday season. I had just finished helping someone and looked up to see John walking into the bank, dressed in his Navy whites. His manly presence took over the lobby. I couldn't deny my attraction to him when he walked up to my window.

"Annie, it's good to see you."

His warm handshake made me blush.

"It's good to see you, John."

"I'm on leave and thought I would try again. How about going out with me? I'm in town for a few days. If you're free, I'd enjoy spending time with you. Are you sure we can't make this happen?"

I hesitated before finally saying, "Yes, I'm sure."

We talked a few more minutes until it was time to say goodbye. My heart sighed as I watched him walk out of my life. I had given him no other choice. When he got to the door, he turned and looked at me one last time. I wanted to run after him but knew I couldn't. I would always wonder if I made the right decision.

More Doubts

I folded the letter from my friend, Pat, who was attending summer school classes at Ohio State. I was upset by her news that Bob had decided to move across town, even though he knew my rooming house was only a block away from him. I wondered when he planned to tell me about his ridiculous decision. Instead of calling him right then, I decided to wait until Thanksgiving to confront him.

He had asked me twice to get my parents' permission to spend the holiday with his family. I knew Mom and Dad would say absolutely not. Seconds after I asked, Dad shut off the television, the kids scattered and Mom turned in her chair. My stomach churned when she said, "You are to be with our family on that day."

"Mom, why does everything I say lead to an argument? Can't you and Dad at least consider it?"

For the next few minutes, they spoke in French. Then Dad said in his familiar blustering tone, "We will let you go over later in the afternoon after we've had our dinner as a family."

I wanted to say, "It's absurd that I need your permission at my age!" But instead said, "Thank you."

When Bob picked me up to go to the movies, I was still on edge. After telling him what my parents said, I changed the topic to my more pressing concern.

"I don't understand why you're moving across town. What happened? You were happy in that apartment."

"Oh, there was too much noise in the hallways. I couldn't study. I found a quieter place that an older couple owns."

"But why? You want me in Columbus and now we're farther away from each other. It doesn't make sense."

"Annie, I told you it's better for me. Besides, we'll still see a lot of each other. I'd rather talk about something else."

"Such as?"

"Such as engagement rings."

An hour later, we were standing in front of a jewelry store that had closed for the day. The window display sparkled with diamonds and outlandish prices. When he asked me what style I liked, I pointed at the emerald cut diamond set in white gold.

He said, "If that is what you want, that is what you'll have. And just so you know, I won't keep you waiting long. I'm proposing on Christmas Eve."

By mid-December, my stomach was continually upset and I was so nervous that I had trouble staying on task at work. I was terrified of Dad's inevitable reaction to the engagement. He had told us several times to wait and not get married. It was an order and not a request. Bob didn't care. He told me repeatedly that he loved me and things would work out. I wasn't so sure. Even though he made me feel special when we were together, it bothered me that we saw so little of each other. I knew he spent a lot of time studying but he could have at least called occasionally. I sometimes felt like an afterthought in his life.

Then there was John. I remembered every detail of that day when he walked into the bank. My heart said, "Do it. Go out with him!" while my mind said, "You can't. You promised to be faithful to Bob."

On my walk home, I tried to appreciate the street lights decorated with garland and the holiday music playing from the city hall. It was Christmas Eve and I should have been filled with joy instead of worry. I was actually hoping that Bob changed his mind about proposing. It was the only way to avoid a terrible confrontation with Dad.

When I walked in the house and saw the pot roast dinner, I tried to sound calm and believable.

"Mom, thank you for all of this. I'm looking forward to this evening. Is there anything I can do to help?"

"Not really. It's ready. Your dad should be here any minute."

After he got home, I helped carry the food to the table and let everyone know it was time to eat. The kids ran down the stairs and took their seats, waiting patiently for Dad to say the prayer. I was thankful that he seemed to be in a relatively good mood.

After we finished, I cleared the table and helped clean up the kitchen. Dad grabbed his coat and said, "Marguerite, I'll be back. I need to take care of a few details at the church. I'll pick you up in 30 minutes."

I went to my bedroom to freshen up before going with Bob to his church service. When the doorbell rang, I rushed down the steps and shouted, "I'll get it!"

I opened the door and cheerfully said, "Merry Christmas!"

He smiled and kissed me. I breathed in the scent of his English Leather. He looked so handsome in his dark suit and long tweed coat. Relief surged through me when I saw that he wasn't holding anything in his hand.

We sat down on the sofa and he told me about his day. I could hear Mom putting things away in the kitchen. She stopped working a few times, trying to hear our conversation. I closed my eyes in anticipation of what Bob might say as he moved closer and put his arm around me.

"Annie, even though your dad isn't going to be happy, we might as well get this over with."

He reached into his coat pocket and pulled out a tiny box wrapped in silver paper with a small red bow. He laid it in my palm and said, "Will you marry me?"

My hands shook as I untied the ribbon. I stared at the enticing white box before lifting the lid that revealed a blue velvet box inside. I gently picked it up as if it were fragile. Inside was a gorgeous emerald cut diamond ring. It was smaller than the one in the store window but that didn't matter.

"Oh, it's beautiful! Yes, I'll marry you!"

The ring fit perfectly. He quickly said, "I'm sorry it's not as big as the one we looked at but it was too expensive. One day, I'll buy you a larger one."

"Bob, I love it. I want to show Mom."

She was drying the dishes when I stood beside her, held up my hand and said, "Look what I got for Christmas."

She turned away and said, "Your father will be furious. What are you thinking?"

I walked back into the living room. He could tell from my expression that things hadn't gone well.

"We'll be okay, Annie. I love you."

A few minutes later, Dad got home. When he came in the back door, he and Mom started talking quickly in French. Bob held me even closer. I stared at the floor when he walked into the room. Instead of yelling, he smiled and said, "I hear you have something to tell me."

I got up and held out my hand. He looked me in the eye and said, "Congratulations. I'm happy for you and Bob." He hugged me, kissed me on the cheek and muttered, "Very nice."

Bob stood up, shook hands and accepted his congratulations. It was surreal when Dad said, "You kids have a nice evening. Enjoy the church service. I know you have to go. Merry Christmas."

Mom came out of the kitchen and said, "Bob, I wish your family a Merry Christmas."

Once we were on the porch, I felt like I could finally breathe.

"I'm still in shock how my parents reacted. I can't wait to show my ring to everyone at church."

We were inseparable for the next two days. It was wonderful spending so much time together without any disagreements or hearing him say, "I need to get back. I have so much to do." We spent the entire weekend with both of our families. It meant so much to me that Mom and Dad went out of their way to make him feel comfortable. Before falling asleep each night, I thanked God for such a peaceful, joyous Christmas.

I was eager to go back to work on Monday and share the exciting news with my co-workers. As I started to walk out the door, Dad bellowed from the kitchen, "You aren't going anywhere! Sit down. NOW!"

When I turned and saw his formidable figure in the middle of the living room, I put my coat on the back of the chair and dropped down on the sofa. As he walked towards me, I felt trapped. He bent down, pointed his finger in my face and yelled, "You have disgraced our family by going against our wishes. We told you not to get engaged. We're ashamed of you and your actions!"

When I started to stand up and defend myself, he yelled even louder, "Sit back down!"

I looked up at him as tears slid down my cheeks.

"Why did you congratulate us? You gave us your blessing and you acted happy for me. What has changed?"

"Look at me. Do you think I was going to spoil Christmas for the rest of the family?"

"Then why did you allow me to date him all these years?"

"We hoped when you went away to college that you would fall for someone else. You are too young. He isn't the right one for you. You've embarrassed us."

"How can you say that? I have never embarrassed you. I've lived by your rules all my life. I never did a thing to hurt you. I never got pregnant and I was never in trouble."

Mom stared at me with her hands on her hips and said, "Well, my dear, if he is the one you choose, you've made your bed. Now lie in it! Life is not a bed of roses. Don't expect us to help you. Do not ask for money. We have others to think of. We are so disappointed in you."

As they started to turn their backs on me, Dad said, "You reap what you sow!"

They might as well have said, "Get out of this house and never come back!"

I sat alone and cried. I would never forget their hurtful words.

Several minutes later, Mom called out, "Go now or you'll be late for work."

I was unsteady when I stood up and grabbed the arm of the chair before going to the bathroom. My eyes were bloodshot and my face was smeared with makeup. I looked like I'd been grieving for weeks. After washing and rinsing my face thoroughly, I applied new makeup and layers of powder to conceal my tear-stained cheeks. Knowing my co-workers would ask about my red nose and swollen eyes, I'd have to tell them it was allergies or a bad cold. It would be easier to lie than tell the truth.

I left the house without saying anything. I felt so unloved. Thankfully, Bob wanted me in his life. Otherwise, I had no place to go.

Independence

I packed as much as possible in the Chevy station wagon, knowing that I wouldn't be returning home anytime soon. Since my parents were barely speaking to me, the drive to Columbus was uncomfortably long. Had there been any opportunity for a civil conversation, I would have explained Columbus Business University's excellent credentials and reputation. I would have told them that in nine months, I could complete the private secretarial program that would be impressive on my resume.

They made it very clear that they would only pay the $40 monthly dorm fee. The rest was up to me. Fortunately, I saved over $900 while working at the bank, which more than covered my tuition. While I was grateful for the job, I knew I couldn't work there for the rest of my life. It was tedious many days and the only way to move up would have involved in-depth training. I knew that I lacked the math and comprehension skills that were required. More than anything, I wanted to be with Bob.

The dorm was a two-story house that sat on the corner of a busy one-way street north of Columbus. The traffic buzzed by as Dad pulled into a parking space in front of it. They quickly helped me get things from the car and carried them to my newly decorated room in the basement. I was hurt by Mom's sarcastic goodbye when she said, "Well, I hope you are happy here."

In February, she called and abruptly said, "Annie, we will be moving soon. Dad has a new job. If you want your personal belongings, come home and get them or we will throw everything out."

"I don't have time to come home. Mom, please keep my pictures in the box and the mementos on my bulletin board. You can give the dresses to my sister or donate them."

I struggled to stay interested in the business classes. They reminded me of high school and were nothing like my courses at OSU. The sessions weren't challenging but they were time consuming. I was bored with many of the repetitive assignments and as a result, I had trouble staying interested. It would have been nice to vent my frustrations to Bob who claimed he was too busy with school and work to see much of me. I questioned how sincere he was each time he said how much he missed me. I unloaded my feelings one night, whether he had time for me or not.

"My roommate's boyfriend is busy but he makes an effort to spend time with her. Why can't you at least call me? I've sacrificed a lot to be near you and I'm starting to wonder why."

He got angry and cut me off. "You know my schedule is rough. I have to study harder than most students because my classes are difficult. Your friend's classes are obviously not as demanding as mine."

I couldn't believe his callous tone.

"That's not fair and you know it. I envy how Ken finds time for Jill. If you lived closer, we could be at your apartment and have some privacy. You keep telling me that you can't live without me. If that's true, why did you move?"

"How many times do I have to tell you? I couldn't study in that other place. I needed more space and the price was right. That's all. We'll be married soon. By the way, did you visit the doctor yet? You'll need to ask about the pill. It's a new form of birth control that you'll need to get on by July at least. The last thing we need is for you to get pregnant. I have a doctor's number if you haven't made your appointment."

I resented that he talked down to me and said, "Thanks, but I'll see my doctor in June."

There were several details that I needed to take care of before the wedding, so I was glad to receive a letter from the pastor who shared important information.

April 29, 1966
Dear Annie,

Your dad tells me that you would like to be married in our church this summer. If he gave me the desired date, I've forgotten it. We require premarital counseling. Since this is difficult for you because of the distance involved, I have taken the liberty of making arrangements for marriage counseling at a church in Columbus. They are willing to give you the necessary advice.

It has been my experience that couples who plan to attend church after they are married rarely do. It seems to drag on and becomes a painful subject. I would strongly recommend that you begin thinking about which church you would like to join individually before marriage. I would welcome a chance to correspond with you in this regard.

Since I'm working "in the dark" about your wedding date and other plans, I've had to make certain presuppositions based on what your dad told me. Let me know what you would like.

Sincerely,
Pastor John

I appreciated his gesture and was certainly receptive to the counseling. I hoped Bob would be too. Instead, he was condescending.

"Annie, I don't have time for this nonsense. We've been together for a long time and we don't need counseling."

"Bob, if we don't go, we can't get married in either church."

It was a struggle to convince him but we finally attended a couple of sessions with a pastor in Columbus. Even though Bob insisted that he couldn't make the final one, the pastor signed the paperwork that we had completed the requirements.

As summer approached, he talked about getting a job in Columbus. I was delighted and looked forward to his help in planning the wedding. When he picked me up one evening in his new Chevy Corvair, I was anxious to hear about his job search. After a quick kiss, he nonchalantly said, "Honey, my plans have changed. I have to do my internship in Sparta, Ohio. It's a great opportunity but it means I'll be spending the summer away."

"What did you say? I thought you wanted us to be together and now you plan to leave town. I don't get it. I'm here in Columbus because that's what you wanted."

"Hey, it's in our best interest. I'll come back to see you whenever I can. I need the internship to graduate and I'll get a little pay on the side. You need to save as much as you can this summer too. We'll need the extra cash."

"If it's in our best interest, you should have discussed it with me before making the decision. My opinions should matter to you but they don't. I'll try to save some money but you know my schedule. I have classes in the morning and work at the bank in the afternoons. My job doesn't pay well. I barely make enough to pay for food and necessities. You've thrown a lot of discouraging news at me tonight. As big as Columbus is, I have a hard time believing that you couldn't find an internship here. And why is money such a pressing issue now?"

His only response was to kiss me and say, "I love you." Normally, I would give in whenever he said that but it was different this time. He disregarded my feelings completely and showed no regret. I couldn't help but question his behavior.

Opinions

He didn't honor his promise to come see me and always had excuses. The most popular one was saying that he needed to work on the weekends. When I found out that wasn't true and questioned him about it, he claimed that he was too far away to drive back and forth.

"Annie, we need to save money for school and not waste it on gasoline."

Planning for the wedding led to one dispute after another. His family wanted a big affair at the reception with alcohol and dancing. Dad said, "They both go against my family's values." Bob wanted a photographer who Dad thought was too expensive. He wouldn't give in, even after I told him Bob's parents would pay for it. Dad shook his head and said, "No. That's final."

Because Bob wasn't intimidated by Dad in the least, he told me to schedule the photographer anyhow. I resented being caught in the middle of the conflicts, especially when it involved where we'd get married. Mom and I wanted the service to be in our church with our minister but Bob was against it. When I finally gave in, we decided to marry in his church with both of our ministers officiating. The next conflict centered on the date for the wedding. Bob preferred having it in the summer but Dad disagreed. After several arguments, they settled on September 10th. The date was so close to school starting that there wouldn't be much time for a honeymoon.

His parents insisted on having the reception at the Elks hall. I knew that would never happen. Dad insisted that it would be in the church fellowship hall right after the service and would be catered by the church women. When Bob objected, Dad looked at me and said, "Annie, if you don't agree with me, marry someone else."

Bob returned to Sparta a few days later. It was several weeks until I heard from him again and then one Friday evening, he called me unexpectedly and said, "Hey, I can come home this weekend."

"Wonderful! I can't wait to see you. I'll pack a picnic."

It was a perfect day, complete with swimming in the lake. I reveled in his warm affection, as he wrapped a towel around my shivering body and gently kissed the back of my neck and shoulders. I made the mistake of assuming we'd be together the entire weekend, so I was disheartened when he left the next day.

On Monday morning, I woke up in pain. When I went to the bathroom, it was so severe that I doubled over. I dialed Bob's number.

"Hello."

"Bob, I'm in terrible pain."

"Listen, I don't have time to talk. I'm at work."

"Please, just give me a minute."

After I told him my symptoms, he said, "Call a doctor. It sounds like you have a urinary tract infection. I have to go. Goodbye."

I bent over in agony while racing through the phone book, trying to find the name of the doctor who my friends recommended. After I talked to the receptionist, she told me to come in right away. I walked several blocks to his office, stopping often to catch my breath. After the examination, the doctor said, "You have a urinary tract infection. I'm writing a prescription for some medicine that will take care of it. Drink a lot of water and rest as much as you can."

I waited every evening for Bob to call and check on me but the phone never rang.

Help

The girls were gone for summer vacation and I was by myself in the large house. While they were enjoying their busy lives, mine was consumed with turmoil. My parents were ashamed of me and Bob put his wants ahead of mine. Why had I sacrificed so much for a man who said he loved me but rarely demonstrated it?

The nagging questions wore me down to the point where I couldn't sleep and had no appetite. I was eaten up by the stress and paid the price. I woke up one morning with a severe sore throat and was unable to keep food down. It took what little strength I had to get to the phone in the hall and call my boss at work.

"This is Annie. I can't come in. I'm very ill."

I crawled back into bed with my clothes on and slept several hours. The next day, I felt worse and called my parents. Dad was concerned and said, "We're on our way. Be ready to go when we get there."

I crawled to my dresser and pulled out clothes that I shoved into a paper bag. When they arrived, I needed help getting to the car. We'd only driven a few miles when I gagged and felt like throwing up. Mom turned to the backseat and said, "Are you pregnant?"

"No! I'm sick!"

The doctor saw me right away and said, "No wonder you feel terrible.

You have acute tonsillitis. I'll write a prescription and you'll need complete bed rest for a week."

"But I have a job."

"If you don't rest, you will not get better."

When I became violently ill after taking the medication, the doctor determined that I was allergic to the sulfa drug and started me on a new prescription. I was in bed for almost two weeks. I found out later that Bob called. Mom said he insisted on speaking to me but she told him I was too sick and wouldn't allow it. He called again a week later and said, "May I please speak with Annie?"

"No. You don't have the decency to come and see her or send a card. I will not get my daughter." She said it so loudly that I could hear everything.

After 10 days had passed, she stood at the foot of my bed and said, "You better get up soon or we will call off the wedding."

From her perspective, his actions warranted canceling it.

"Mom, he has so much to do. Please leave it alone."

After she left, I forced myself to get dressed. Even though I barely had the strength to eat any dinner or mingle with everyone, I did my best to appear better than I really felt. If I hadn't, Mom and Dad wouldn't let me return to Columbus.

Concern

By the first week of August, I was slowly putting my life back together. It felt good returning to school and work. Everyone was happy to see me. As the weekend approached, my anxiety increased, as I envisioned what it would be like to see Bob again. When he pulled up, I waited for him to come to the door. It was obvious how surprised he was by my appearance.

"Annie, are you okay?"

"I'm better but still need to regain my strength."

"Honey, how much weight have you lost?"

"I'm down to 89 pounds but I guess it's not bad on my 5'2" frame."

He laughed and said, "Listen, if you make it to 100 pounds by the wedding, I'll give you $100."

I wasn't in the mood for his glib remark and removed my engagement ring and put it in his hand.

"I'm concerned about our relationship. Do you still want to get married? You don't seem to feel the same way about me as I do about you. Bob, I'm not sure now if it's the right thing to do."

He put the ring back on my finger.

"Yes, I want to get married because I love you. Please don't be concerned. I'm under a lot of stress with work and school."

His kiss felt sincere. As much as I enjoyed the tender moment, it was tainted when he said, "How much money have you saved?"

"Unbelievable! I haven't been able to work for two weeks. What did you expect me to save? Give me some time. You're the one working, remember? Why aren't you saving more? What's wrong?"

"Nothing is wrong but we might not have enough money."

I took the ring off again and dropped it in his hand. I was tired of it all.

"Yeah, sure, I'll do what I can. Maybe you'd have more money if you had stayed in Columbus."

"Annie, our wedding is in a few more weeks. I can't imagine my life without you. I'm just saying that you need to try harder to put money in your savings account. Please take the ring back."

I nodded half-heartedly and put it on.

A week later, I took a bus to Belden to spend a long weekend with him and his parents. Once we were in the car, his mother asked if I was excited about our appointment with the florist the next day. I smiled and said, "I just hope everything goes well. Thank you for helping with the floral expenses."

I wanted to be excited but was feeling uneasy because Mom was going to join us. When we arrived at the house, Bob's car was in the drive but he didn't come out to greet me. Once inside, he gave me a quick kiss and casually said, "Sorry I didn't pick you up. I had things to do. I hope you understand."

"I do. It's fine."

He showed little interest in the conversations at dinner and was quiet for the rest of the evening. If he was happy to be with me, it didn't show.

When Mom arrived the next day, she greeted us with a polite smile. I wondered how long that would last. Once inside the floral shop, we were ushered to a table. The cordial shop owner said, "These books are filled with pictures of beautiful flowers. Please flip through them to get some ideas. I'll be back shortly to answer your questions."

I already knew what I wanted but joined in the fun and marked my favorite pages. I looked up when Bob's mother said, "Annie, please pick out your bouquet. Don't forget that the flowers are on us."

I hadn't thought of the bouquet and humbly said, "Thank you so much."

When the owner returned, I said, "I've made my decisions."

He took detailed notes of everything I wanted. Then Bob's mother reminded me again about choosing a bouquet. Before I could respond, Bob set a book on the table and said, "How about this one?"

"Oh, that is lovely!" his mother exclaimed. The bride in the picture held a bouquet of orchids that cascaded to the floor.

"This is what you'll carry, Annie. I know you like orchids and this is my gift to you."

"Thank you, Bob. They're stunning."

When we returned to the house, he and his mother thanked Mom for coming and went inside. I stood in the driveway as she got ready to leave. Her mood changed dramatically and she was furious when she said, "His mother spent too much money on those flowers. They make us look bad."

In a pleading tone, I said, "They told you they would pay for everything. Why can't you let them help?"

She barely looked at me and drove off.

When I returned to Columbus, I called her and said, "Mom, would you go with me to pick out my wedding gown? I'd really appreciate your support. I know our family is limited on money and I'm working hard to make the wedding as simple as possible."

She went with me but said very little. I tried on a gown I loved and was so disappointed when the shop assistant said that someone had just purchased it and she couldn't order another one in time. I had no other option but to go with my second choice.

Marriage

I was amused when Mom told me why Dad finally agreed to a September wedding. It was because my grandmother and aunt spoke to him privately and said, "Charlie, you need to ease up. You'll lose your daughter if you continue on this path. Let them get married."

Even though he wasn't happy they interfered, he gave in as much as his stubborn will would allow. What my parents didn't realize is that Bob and I would have run away and gotten married, regardless what they thought. While I wanted their blessing, it wasn't a necessity because they "lost" me on that Monday after Christmas when they shunned me.

One week before the wedding, Bob wanted me to see the mobile home he'd found for us. I was looking so forward to starting our lives together that I didn't question why he made the decision without my input. On the way, he explained that it would provide the privacy he wanted and that one of the rooms would be his alone. His parents were already there when we arrived and had cleaned every inch of it. Freshly ironed curtains framed the windows. After we enjoyed the picnic lunch his mother packed, I thanked them repeatedly for their immense help. For the first time, I could picture us as newlyweds. When his parents left, I reached up to give him a flirtatious kiss and he responded with the affection I sought. He reminded me that there would be plenty more after we were married.

Thanks to our talented wedding coordinator, the rehearsal went well. I especially enjoyed hearing our friend sing the Lord's Prayer so beautifully. I couldn't believe it when Bob said he didn't want him involved in the service, especially since they'd been neighbors for years. It made no sense and I wouldn't go along with it.

Everyone had a wonderful time at the rehearsal dinner that Bob's parents hosted at a banquet center. My parents interacted with everyone and appeared to enjoy themselves. They seemed more relaxed, which made me wonder if they were finally accepting the inevitable. It meant so much to me a few days before the dinner when Mom surprised me with a floral sleeveless dress. I had never felt prettier.

I snuggled up to Bob as we pulled out of the parking lot.

"I had such a great time tonight."

"I did too, Annie."

"I'm so happy. The whole evening was perfect. I love you so much, Bob."

He kissed me and said, "Just think. You'll be my wife tomorrow and we'll be off on our honeymoon."

Then he kissed my neck and said, "Darling, how much money did you save?"

His insensitivity disgusted me and I pushed him away.

"What is wrong with you? We've talked about this before. You know I haven't been able to save much. I haven't been back at work that long."

His mood flipped and he yelled in ire, "How can I go through with this wedding? You don't care about us and our future. We can't go on a honeymoon now because you didn't save the money. You are childish and inconsiderate!"

I slid to the other side of the car in shock and fear. I didn't recognize him. I started crying and said, "I'm sorry you don't understand."

Once he calmed down, he moved closer and said, "Annie, I thought you realized how much we need the extra cash. You know I love you."

I stared into the darkness and said, "Please take me to Pat's house. I'm tired."

He apologized when he dropped me off but it didn't change anything. He had ruined a special night in my life.

When I woke up the next morning, Pat was already gone but her mother had graciously made French toast and bacon for breakfast. I had no appetite, so I picked at my food while we talked about the wedding. I smiled the entire time, disguising how much Bob had upset me.

By the time I got my hair done at the salon and ran a few errands, it was already 5:30 when I pulled up beside the florist's delivery truck in the church parking lot. Warm tears gathered in my eyes when I saw how beautiful the sanctuary looked, complete with pew bows, the candelabra and breathtaking flowers. I turned when a familiar voice said hello.

I smiled at the wedding coordinator and said, "As you can tell by my reaction, the church looks stunning. It's beyond anything I could have ever imagined. Thank you."

"You're welcome. I'm glad you're pleased. Your mother dropped off your wedding dress this afternoon, so let me show you the room where you and the attendants will change."

"I'm afraid I'm early. I wanted to make sure everything was in place."

"That's no problem. This will give me a chance to tell you what we've gotten done and the finishing touches we still need to make."

When we walked into the room, a delivery man was setting a box on the table. The coordinator thanked him as I opened it and breathed in the sweet scents. She nodded in agreement when I said, "These flowers will look gorgeous against the gold and cream fabric of my attendants' gowns. I bought them ivory necklaces that will look exquisite. They should be here soon."

A few minutes later, I could hear their laughter outside the door. I was so thankful for the support of my friends. They talked nonstop and took turns helping with the cloth-covered buttons that streamed down the back of my gown. When it was time for them to change into their dresses, I lifted my bouquet from the box. The rosebuds and gardenias were very pretty but it was so much smaller than the bouquet that Bob promised me. I tried to dismiss it from my mind but wondered if he was aware of it.

When the organist started to play, Mom quietly walked into the room and gave me a much needed hug that settled my nerves. It wasn't long until the coordinator knocked on the door and said, "Annie, it's time."

I fought back the tears when I saw how handsome Dad looked in his tuxedo. As I tucked my arm in his, he kissed my cheek and whispered, "You look lovely." As we slowly walked down the aisle, I was surprised that there were so few people on Bob's side of the church because they expected a large crowd. It was even more obvious compared to my side that was filled with family and friends.

He winked at me when he took my hand and said, "I love you." I didn't know what to think after the minister said, "You may kiss the bride." He kissed me with a passion that made me uncomfortable in front of my parents.

After we stood in the receiving line and thanked everyone for coming, we followed the last of the guests down the steps to the reception area. When it was time to cut the tastefully decorated cake, I wasn't happy when he smashed a piece into my mouth with force. I had no other choice but to clean off my face in the restroom. When I rejoined the festivities, we opened a few gifts, although he seemed more interested in collecting the envelopes and giving the money to his mother for safekeeping.

The reception was scheduled to end at 11 o'clock but I slipped away at 10:30 to change into my two-piece travel suit. I took the small corsage from the center of my bouquet and pinned it to the front of the jacket. My travel bag was already in the car.

Bob wanted to plan our honeymoon, so I looked forward to being surprised. Since he was concerned about the money, I knew we wouldn't be going to the large hotel outside of Toledo. I was baffled, though, when he pulled into a local motel only eight miles away. I didn't say anything when he parked in front of the lobby and said, "I'll be back in a minute. I have to check in."

We drove around to the motel's far side. I picked up my bag and walked to door number 8. When he noticed that I hadn't followed him into the room, he said, "Aren't you coming inside?"

"Oh, I was hoping you'd carry me over the threshold."

He held the door open and laughed. "I'm not picking you up. I could hurt my back."

I didn't let on how disappointed I was and dropped my bag on the bed. I walked towards him, wrapped my arms around his neck and gave him a lingering kiss. He backed away and said, "Go take a shower. It's been a long day."

I was speechless. After I showered, I lathered my body with lotion and put on my seductive negligee. When I walked into the room, he was already in bed and acted like he didn't notice me. Instead of taking me in his arms, he poured two glasses of champagne and made a toast.

"Hey, honey, here's to our beautiful day and our marriage and to whatever the future holds." After that, he went into the bathroom.

When he returned, he crawled into bed and turned off the lights. After we kissed, he rolled over and was soon fast asleep. A waterfall of tears soaked my pillow. I really didn't know this stranger who was lying beside me. He had ruined another special moment in my life.

The next night, I reached over and he pushed me away.

"Annie, I'm tired."

I stared into the darkness and silently prayed. *Dear Lord, I'm so sorry I went astray. Please forgive me. I broke the commandment of honoring my father. He was right about Bob but I didn't listen. I will honor my marriage vows. My life and my future are in your hands.*

Submission

My job at the bank was the same daily routine. I typed stock certificates, entered them in the ledger and filled out the necessary forms that were sent to data processing. Even though it could be tedious, it was better than being home with Bob and putting up with his insults.

Because I fell behind with my classes when I was sick in the summer, I wouldn't graduate until January. Unless I had a night class, I usually got home from work at 6 o'clock and prepared dinner immediately. He rarely emerged from his study until then. We ate in silence while he read the newspaper or studied. When we finished, I rinsed off the dishes and placed them in a pile from the previous days' meals. I wasn't allowed to wash them until the weekend because he said I made too much noise.

I did laundry every three weeks and hauled the baskets home from the laundromat on Saturdays. Whenever I asked if we could attend church before I spent all of Sunday afternoon ironing his clothes, he said that he didn't have time. I often went to bed early out of boredom. One night after I had fallen asleep, he woke me up and said, "You will not go to bed with rollers in your hair. Take them out."

"But how do you expect me to be ready in the morning?"

"Get up an hour earlier."

"You don't pay attention to me anyhow, so it shouldn't matter. Besides, I don't understand why everything has to be your way."

After slamming his fist on the nightstand and swearing at me, he said, "It's my career. I need your cooperation to help me succeed."

The more he studied and ignored me, the more I needed interaction with my friends. I asked multiple times if I could get in touch with them but he always brushed me off and said my conversations with them were silly. It eventually reached a point where he wouldn't let me visit them at all. The phone was off limits, too, because he said the calls distracted him and were too expensive. I felt nauseous when he bought me a pair of earphones to use when I watched TV. His absurd behavior escalated when he set up a folding partition to block any noise that might filter to his room. I prayed daily, asking God to help me survive my suffocating environment.

As the time neared for our first Christmas together, I made up my mind that I was going to decorate, regardless how meager it might look. I couldn't believe it when he came up with the money for a small tree, bulbs and lights. I was even more surprised that he took some time to help me. When he gave me a few dollars to buy him a gift, I purchased a Herb Alpert album because he seemed to enjoy the music when it played in the car.

When he unwrapped it, he said, "Why did you buy this? You like his music but I don't."

Six months into the marriage, I was convinced that I had married an extremely domineering man. It affected me emotionally and physically. Everything I did was wrong, including my cooking, the color of my hair, the way I slept and how I put toilet paper on the roll. When he began making demands one evening after dinner, my throat tightened and my face began to swell. When my eyes were nearly swollen shut, he helped me to bed and brought me some Benadryl. It was the first time I had seen him show any compassion.

That unnerving experience was a turning point for me. I made the conscious decision that I was going to voice my opinions, whether he liked it or not. I couldn't be submissive to his bullying. My sanity and physical well-being depended on it. From that point on, I never had another swelling attack.

Up and Down

It was a relief when I finally received my secretarial degree. Bob only had one more year of school left and I was hopeful that his mood swings would stabilize after he was employed and earning a good income. I was tired of being made to feel guilty if I spent a dime on a Coke or $2 for two pair of shoes. I knew he was under a lot of pressure and the closer he got to graduating, the more nervous he became.

He was against the war in Vietnam and knew that he had to be in school or have a family to avoid being drafted. When he wanted me to have a baby as soon as possible, I stopped taking the pill in the middle of a cycle. We were both disappointed when my period arrived on time each month. One weekend when Bob's parents visited, his mother and I waited in the car while the guys were shopping. I could only contain my excitement so long before I said, "We're trying to have a baby."

I was in utter disbelief when she sighed and said, "I don't think that's a good idea."

I was bothered for weeks by her puzzling response.

After our failed attempts at getting pregnant, Bob got in touch with a friend who explained another way to solve his dilemma. He had terrible bouts with allergies and a trip to the doctor placed him in a 4-F classification. After getting all the forms signed and filed, he received the deferment.

When I arrived home from work one afternoon, I saw a letter on the table from my friend, Sue. The envelope was already opened because Bob had been opening my mail, despite the pleas to quit invading my privacy. He had the audacity to correct Sue's letter by highlighting her grammar errors in red and left this brazen message at the bottom: *She's going to grad school. She should know how to write.*

During his graduation ceremony, I envisioned walking across that same stage one day. While I was proud of him, I kept thinking about the arrogant comment he made a few months earlier when he said, "Annie, you'll have to go back to school when I finish. You won't be in the same league with me if you don't."

"I can't believe some of the things you say, Bob. I know women who don't plan to go on to school. My friend, Nancy, isn't going to college and her husband accepts and appreciates her. You have no right to speak to me like that."

Support

When he informed me that we'd be moving to Mansfield, Ohio, for his new job, I didn't question it. Mom had taught me to be supportive of decisions made by the man of the house, if it was beneficial to his career. So in four short days, I packed everything and we moved into a nice mobile home park that was nestled among large oak trees.

As refreshing as it was to see him in good spirits, I was dumbfounded by his impulsive behavior, particularly when he bought a used Mercury convertible and a new VW convertible. I was further confused when he shopped for new clothes. He certainly wasn't acting like the old Bob who obsessed over unnecessary spending. I never questioned it because he was making good money.

He was insistent that I enroll at the Mansfield branch of Ohio State University as soon as possible. I welcomed the opportunity because it put me one step closer to my dream of graduating. Even though I took fewer than 15 credits a quarter, I studied nonstop while he worked overtime. As a result, we had little opportunity to spend time together. Consequently, we had fewer arguments.

Shortly after we moved, he decided to buy a new mobile home. I thought living in an apartment might be better but he disagreed. We ended up designing and decorating it ourselves and when it arrived, we were pleased with the final product. For the first time in our marriage, I had a washer and dryer, dishwasher, and a built-in desk that Bob designed for me. Although I enjoyed the new home and the upscale lifestyle, it bothered me that he was never satisfied and always wanted more. When he said he wanted to move to Houston, Texas, I thought he was joking until I found out that he checked into my attending Rice University. A few days later, he changed his mind again and said we were staying. I never understood why he continually wanted to relocate.

I really struggled during the fall quarter with my algebra class. He knew it and yet he said one evening, "Why don't you change your major to pharmacy?"

"What? I'm barely passing my math class. I could never complete a pharmacy program."

"I could help you."

"I'm just not interested, Bob. I've always wanted to be a teacher. That's my passion."

"You know, Annie, I have more in common with my co-workers than I do with you."

After an intense argument, I walked away and went to bed. I kept thinking about some of his co-workers and wondered how many of them were women. I did everything possible not to let my mind go there.

I was filling out the Mansfield OSU form for the spring quarter when he came home from work and said, "Don't finish it. You won't be attending the branch here. We're heading back to Columbus and you can attend the main campus."

"We're moving again? We've only lived here for eight months."

"Yes, we're moving again. Don't question me. Why should it matter to you?"

He never did explain why he was leaving his job. I didn't bother asking because I wasn't sure I'd get the truth.

My Blessing

The decision for us to return to the Columbus area was a good one. Bob took a job at a local pharmacy and I commuted to OSU. I was friends with several girls on campus and thoroughly enjoyed the neighbors in our mobile home park.

Shortly before taking a break from studying one afternoon, Bob handed me quite a bit of money and encouraged me to go shopping for a sexy negligee. I was pleasantly surprised and bought a black two-piece camisole that was alluring and relatively inexpensive. When I put it on and walked into the living room, he picked me up, swung me around and carried me on his shoulder. Instead of going to our bedroom, he turned into the bathroom, lowered me into the tub and walked away.

"Bob, what are you doing?"

"Hey, cool off. I have a football game to watch."

He seemed to enjoy humiliating me. He might as well have said, "I'm not attracted to you." Even though I was used to his rude behavior, this was extra hurtful. He mocked my femininity. I was determined not to give him the satisfaction of knowing it bothered me, so I climbed out of the tub and started studying. It was hard to believe that my life had been reduced to this after three long years of marriage.

He surprised me on Valentine's Day by getting a reservation at a fancy restaurant. He was in a romantic mood the entire evening and didn't complain about anything. It was the most attentive he had ever been to me. His attraction continued in the bedroom but when I woke up the next morning, he had returned to his old self. I knew the timing of my menstrual cycle and had a feeling that I'd become pregnant.

A few weeks later, I fixed a special meal to celebrate the good news I had for him. He looked at me and said, "What's the occasion? Why did you spend money on this expensive cut of meat?"

"I have some good news. I know this might be a little early and a bit of a shock, but I think I'm pregnant. I missed my period."

He stopped eating and didn't change expression when he said, "I know a doctor. I'll call tomorrow and schedule an appointment."

With that, he took a slice of apple pie into the living room and watched TV. We spoke to each other very little the rest of the week.

I went alone to my doctor's appointment. When the nurse sensed how scared I was, she calmly explained the procedure and handed me a sheet to cover my body after I undressed. The next step was to provide a urine sample. I was sitting on the edge of the examining table when the doctor walked in and introduced himself. Although the exam wasn't pleasant, it didn't take long. After I got dressed, he returned to the room and said, "Yes, I do believe by the outward signs that you are with child, but we'll send the test to the lab for confirmation. Please call the office in a few days to get the results. If you are pregnant, you'll come in once a month for exams and will need to take special vitamins. Since you are petite, I won't want you to gain more than 15 pounds during your pregnancy. I'll monitor you carefully. Do you have any questions?"

"Yes, when do you think I'll deliver?"

"From what you've told me and based on the exam, I think you'll deliver close to the 11th of November."

When I got in the car, I bowed my head and thanked Jesus for this wonderful gift. When Bob got home from work, his first words were, "What did the doctor say? It was a false alarm, wasn't it?"

"Not really. He's pretty sure I'm pregnant but we need to wait for the results to be confirmed. I have to call the office in a couple of days."

He was silent while he ate dinner. I quietly waited for him to finish because I wasn't allowed to clear the dishes until he was done. He didn't like extra movement or noise while he ate. I could barely concentrate on my studies the next few days. If he thought he could dampen my spirits by not talking to me, it didn't work. When I called the doctor's office, the nurse gave me the good news immediately.

"Yes, the results are positive. You are pregnant and you're due on the 11th of November."

"Thank you! I'll see you in a few weeks."

After I hung up, I called Bob and my parents right away.

"Bob, it's confirmed. I'm pregnant!"

"Oh, that's great news. I'm happy. I'll see you later."

I prepared a celebration dinner, complete with a T-bone steak, baked potatoes and a scalloped corn dish. When he walked in and didn't sit down to eat, my heart sank. He was clearly upset.

"Annie, we need to talk. Listen to me carefully. We can't have this baby right now."

"How can you say such a horrible thing? I know what you're implying and it breaks my heart. What is wrong with you? You were happy when I told you the news on the phone. We're married and expecting a child from this union. Doesn't that mean anything to you?"

When he came closer, I backed away and yelled, "My dad was right! You don't know what love is. Why did you marry me?"

He didn't say anything until I walked to the phone and started to dial.

"Who are you calling? Annie, put down the phone. I mean it."

He reached for the receiver but it was too late.

"Hello."

My hands were shaking when I said in distress, "Dad, I need your help. Bob isn't happy that I'm pregnant. Please come."

"I'll be right there."

I had barely hung up when Bob yelled, "I can't believe you called him."

I stared at the floor and sobbed.

He walked away and slammed the door in his room. After I picked up his plate full of food, scraped it into the garbage and washed the dishes, I prayed. *Oh, Lord, give me the courage to tell Dad what's happened.*

I sat down on the couch and took long, deep breaths, trying to control my emotions. A few minutes later, I was frightened when I heard Bob's footsteps. I worried that an intense quarrel could cause me to miscarry. When he walked into the living room and started to sit down beside me, I scooted away. A handful of seconds passed before he reached for my trembling hands.

"Annie, I'm sorry about my reaction. I'm still in shock about the baby. I'm just not ready but we'll make it work. I'm sorry you had to call your father and make him drive over here."

"It was okay a couple of years ago to get pregnant when it was your idea but today it isn't. You don't make any sense and I think you're putting on a big act right now because you're afraid of Dad."

He let go of my hands and said, "Let's not argue. I love you."

When Dad arrived, I hoped that he would burst into the room and rip Bob apart. Instead, he spoke calmly. I couldn't believe it. How could he have missed the desperate tone in my voice when I said I needed him?

"I hear there's a problem. Let's sit at the table and talk about it. What's going on, Annie?"

Through my tears, I said, "We've been arguing about the pregnancy. He doesn't want me to have the baby. He's only focused on me finishing my education. He thinks the baby would be an obstacle and inconvenience."

Bob never said a word in response. He was trying to make it appear that he was the mature one in our marriage. Dad was duped by him. I was sure of it when he leaned forward and said, "Annie, sometimes things happen that change the course of our lives. I was in college when the war broke out and I enlisted. I got married and you came along sooner than Marguerite and I anticipated. There were some tough times but we got through them together. We made things work and so can the two of you."

I resented his patronizing words. At the very least, I wanted him to say, "Your mother and I tried to talk you out of marrying him. Now you're living with the consequences."

When he stood up, I knew he was done. There was no point in my saying more. Even though I was dismayed, we hugged and I thanked him for coming. As soon as his car pulled away, Bob turned on the TV and I went to bed. I laid my hand on my belly and praised God. *Lord, thank you for this miracle growing inside me. Please stay with me through whatever lies ahead.*

Motherhood

When it became apparent that the mobile home would be too small once the baby arrived, Bob found a nice townhouse to rent in a suburb outside of Columbus. Even though it only had two bedrooms, I liked having a walk-in closet in the master bedroom, a full basement and a fenced patio. Another perk was having a relatively close commute to OSU.

Our family members were very helpful when it was time to set up a nursery. My grandmother gave us her old rocker and baby bed and my in-laws got us a cradle. I was thankful for everything, including all of the essentials that Mom bought. When I told Bob that we needed to start thinking about baby names, he ignored me until I started mentioning some of my favorites. He interrupted and said, "We won't talk about girls' names because it will be a boy."

During a routine appointment, my doctor explained that he wanted us to participate in Lamaze classes to prepare for the birth. I couldn't bring myself to tell him that Bob thought they'd be a waste of time, so I said, "I'd like to but my husband can't get time off from work. Please just give me information to read."

After the nursery was complete, he was noticeably restless and moody. He finally admitted that he was really upset about not being accepted to law school. It didn't end there. He somehow blamed me for it. For the sake of the baby, I let it go, even though I had a feeling there was more bad news to come.

My instincts were right. The following week, he said, "I'm taking a job in Cleveland. The market is saturated with pharmacists here. I need to go somewhere else. I have an offer to work as a pharmacist and manager in a drugstore. The money is better. I start on November 3rd, so I hope you have the baby before the 11th."

"Are you saying that I won't finish my degree at OSU like we've planned? I thought that was important to you. I only have a year to go. You wanted to come back to Columbus and now we're leaving again. What are you doing?"

"Well, I'm not going to be in law school, so what does it matter? You can get your degree in Cleveland. You're the one who wanted this baby, so we'll do what I think is best for our family."

It wasn't worth a heated exchange. If I had responded, I would have said, "Who are you kidding? You're not thinking about me and the baby. You're doing what is best for you."

In addition to the Cleveland offer, he also had an opportunity to work in a small town in northwestern Ohio. One Sunday morning, he said, "Let's take a trip to see what it's like before I make my final decision. We'll take the VW. Maybe the bumpy ride will bring on labor pains."

Even though I was a little uncomfortable in the cramped space, the day went well. I fell in love with the town and said, "This would be a great place to raise a family."

Much to my surprise, he agreed. "Yes, I think it could be a good choice."

Several days later, however, he said, "I've decided we're going to Cleveland."

On the last day of October, I was lying on the sofa reading a book and felt changes in my belly. The baby hadn't moved as much as the previous week and that worried me. The doctor reassured me that the baby wasn't ready to deliver. Bob was more nervous about the move and told me repeatedly, "The baby has to come. We have to give the movers a date."

Two days later, I felt fine and had a lot of energy. As usual, I fixed his lunch for work while he finished breakfast. After he left, I reached up to set a bowl in the cupboard when I felt something trickle down my leg. The next thing I knew, a surge of water hit the floor. I tried to remain calm and dialed the doctor's office. When I told the receptionist what happened, she said, "You should get to the hospital."

I frantically called Bob.

"My water broke. Get me to the hospital!"

"Okay. I'll have to get someone to replace me. I'll be home as soon as I can."

"Hurry!" I cried.

When I started up the stairs to change clothes, there was a stabbing pain in my side. I grabbed the railing for support and cried, "Help me, Jesus!" Once it subsided, I called my parents to let them know I was headed to the hospital.

New Life

When Bob arrived, I was bent over in pain. After helping me to the car, he put my suitcase in the backseat and drove as fast as possible. Once we took the exit off the freeway, I was relieved to see the hospital. When he pulled into a parking lot, I yelled, "Are you kidding? The emergency entrance is over there. I'm having a baby!"

"The walk will do you good. It will make the baby come faster."

I was in too much distress to argue. I put my hand under my belly and took as many steps as I could, having to stop frequently from the pain. He walked ahead with the suitcase and never offered to help me. Fortunately, an ER attendant saw me struggling and quickly came out with a wheelchair. He said, "Why didn't you pull up to the ER? Your wife is in labor."

Bob didn't acknowledge the comment and began filling out the paperwork while I was transported to my room. As the nurse helped me into a gown and inserted an IV in my arm, I asked why several others were standing so close to my bed. I was more than surprised when she said, "This is a teaching hospital. We hope you don't mind if the students observe the birthing process."

I felt good for several hours because the contractions were far apart and the pain was mild. That all changed when the nurse examined me to see how things were progressing. The first time I shrieked in pain, she calmly said, "It will be okay. Breathe like you did in your Lamaze classes."

"No, I didn't take them. Please show me what to do."

After several hours of discomfort, I was given a saddle block. Soon afterwards, I looked at the nurse and said, "The baby is coming. I feel the pressure. I need to push."

"Your doctor is on his way. Hang on just a little bit longer."

Once he finally arrived, the baby didn't move when he told me to push. After more failed attempts, he performed an episiotomy. When the baby still wouldn't come, he looked at the nurse and said, "Get the forceps."

The next thing I knew, the doctor said, "You have a perfect baby girl."

When she began to cry, it was the sweetest sound I'd ever heard. Thankful tears streamed down my face when he said, "Your daughter weighs 6 pounds 1 ounce and is 21 inches long. She was born at 4:34 p.m."

The nurse wrote down the information and placed a pretty pink card in front of the bassinet. When Bob walked in, he handed me a small stuffed animal, a miniature white toy poodle with a red ribbon around its neck. He smiled and said, "Here is the baby's first gift."

I smiled back. "I'm sorry you didn't get your boy. We don't have a girl's name."

"That's okay. You're both well. I'll see you later in your room and we'll talk about it."

After he left, the nurse laid my daughter in my arms. I kissed her gently and whispered, "I will love you forever."

A few minutes later, I handed her back to the nurse, in order for the doctor to stitch my incision. Once I returned to my room, Bob sat down beside my bed. When I started talking about girls' names, he said, "I like the name Cindy with your middle name. I want it to be Cindy Marie."

I thought it sounded cute and said, "What about Cynthia Marie and we'll call her Cindy? Cynthia Marie sounds like a melody. It flows."

"Yes, that will be fine. I wish I could stay longer but I can't. I'll be in Cleveland tomorrow. The company needs me. They'll pay for my stay at a motel until I find a place to live. Mom and Dad will watch our dogs until you're on your feet. If I find something, we'll hopefully move Thanksgiving weekend."

He kissed my cheek and was gone, without ever holding our daughter.

For the next seven days, I walked the halls and prayed that I would be a good mother. I loved counting Cindy's tiny toes and gliding my fingers over her soft skin. The bruises from the forceps were almost gone but the scar under her chin would remain forever.

I had just finished feeding her when my parents walked in. Mom held out her arms and said, "I need to hold our little one."

It was such a memorable moment that I hesitated to interrupt. I stuttered and said, "Is-is it possible for you to take me home when I'm discharged? Bob is in Cleveland."

Mom looked confused.

"Are you saying that he couldn't wait to move until you were home?"

"He started his new job and they're short-handed."

It was apparent from her expression that she thought it was a lame excuse.

The warm sun felt so good on my face when I left the hospital. I only gained 14 pounds with the pregnancy and even though I had lost most of the baby weight, I appreciated the comfort of my maternity dress. I looked at Cindy and said, "We're going home, baby girl."

I had no qualms about being a new mother, after one of the nurses showed me how to feed, change and bathe her. Mom stayed with me for a week. I was so grateful and couldn't imagine what I would have done without her. When Bob came home for the weekend, he held Cindy long enough to have his picture taken. When I questioned why he didn't pick her up again, he said, "I'm afraid I'll break her." He never once volunteered to feed her or change her diaper. At that point, I realized how little help he'd be, other than making sure I had enough formula and diapers for the week.

When he was ready to return to Cleveland on Sunday, he said, "Remember, you have to get this place packed by Thanksgiving. I won't be around to help."

It didn't matter if I was physically up to it or not.

Family Support

My parents watched Cindy over the Thanksgiving weekend when we moved into a house that looked like all the other houses in the subdivision. It was the only rental Bob could find that accepted pets. The positives were having more living space and bedrooms on the first floor.

One morning during breakfast, I approached him about getting Cindy baptized, even though I knew he wouldn't be receptive. He never looked up and grumbled, "I don't have time."

"Then you'll need to make the time. She needs to be baptized and brought up in church. Our families have been asking when it will be."

He reluctantly said, "Well, we can start attending church in Berea. That's not far. I'll talk to someone today. But you aren't a Lutheran and you'll have to take classes first."

"Thank you. I'll call tomorrow and see how soon I can start."

When the cold winter months arrived, Bob's mood swings increased. He complained constantly about being tired and was critical of the help at work. While staring at the TV one night, he said, "Honey, I want you to go back to school and finish your degree. I've investigated colleges in the area. Baldwin Wallace is in Berea and offers a program in your major. They'd like you to call tomorrow. Ask them about your credits and see how long it will take you to graduate. Start checking the newspaper for babysitters. I'll pay your way. I'm afraid if you don't do this now, you might never go back. It's important for your future and our family."

I never knew what he'd expect of me next. He initially was supportive of my wishes to stay home and be a full-time mother and housewife. He offered no explanation why he changed his mind and showed no sympathy when I tearfully said, "I can't bear the thought of leaving her."

I didn't make an appointment with the college admissions clerk for several days. When I finally did meet with her, she said, "We'll accept your classwork but you'll have to repeat a course. You'll need to take the Home Management class."

"But I was required to take this class at OSU. They waived it because I was married and pregnant. I'm a mother now. Doesn't that count for something? I've also been keeping house for four years. I'm disappointed that this department is so far behind the times."

When I got home, I sat on the couch and prayed for several minutes before picking up the phone to ask my parents for help again. When Mom answered, I said, "I hate to ask for a favor but I have a problem with my course schedule. If you can't watch Cindy because of your hysterectomy, just let me know."

"Annie, I'm much better. I hate that you have to go through this but I'll be glad to help."

"But I have to stay in that house for six weeks, Mom. I'm required to be there from 7:30 a.m. to 8 p.m."

"That's fine. We'll look after her. Since it's that long, I think it would be best for her to stay with us the whole time and not transport her back and forth. Infants do better with a routine."

Being separated from her was the most stressful time in my life. I missed her so much that I ached all over. I buried myself in school work and avoided going into her bedroom. I felt like a terrible mother and was determined that I would make it up to her after I graduated in the summer. I called once a week to see how things were going. She was doing fine and enjoyed my brothers entertaining her. Bob never asked how she was getting along. He was absorbed in working as many hours as he could that included weekends.

As soon as I completed the six-week course, Mom and Dad brought her home. She quickly headed to the toys lying on the floor. I expected her to smile when I leaned over to pick her up but she shied away. So I got down on my knees and played with her until she reached out to be held. While it took some time getting reacquainted, she had my undivided attention.

Along with all the school work, I was completing the sessions at church to become a Lutheran. Six months later, Cindy was baptized. Bob wanted to keep the ceremony simple and not invite family members. Even though I was disappointed that our families wouldn't be there, I took solace in knowing she was in God's hands. I was also pleased that we had a church home.

Our lease was up in November and it didn't take him long to find a new three-bedroom home on one level that wasn't far from his workplace. The move meant finding a new babysitter and attending another church in Parma. After searching the newspaper, I found a kind lady who took care of other children. The experience went well but by the time Cindy was two years old, I knew she needed more social interaction and I enrolled her in daycare.

Before graduating, students majoring in education were asked to complete paperwork that indicated their preferred school districts. I looked at my counselor and spoke honestly.

"Ms. Shaw, I plan to stay home and raise my daughter. I'm not going to teach right away."

"I understand, Annie, but it's one of our requirements. Please go ahead and fill out the information."

Little did I know at the time how crucial that paperwork would be.

Unexpected

We had moved so many times that it would have been laughable if it weren't so frustrating. When new homes were still going up in our neighborhood, Bob said, "I've decided that we're going to look at the models and build one."

While the construction was underway, I received an important phone call. The gentleman said, "Hello, this is Assistant Superintendent Brown. I'm calling to ask if you would be interested in a part-time teaching position. You come highly recommended."

"Thank you. Could you please give me more details?"

"Yes. We need to fill a position for a teacher going on maternity leave. We need an answer today because school starts tomorrow."

"I appreciate the offer but I need to discuss this with my husband. I'll call you back in a few minutes."

Bob was in his study. I knocked on the door and asked if I could come in.

"I just got a phone call from a school district in need of a part-time teacher. If I take it, I'll be able to make over $3,000 and would have my foot in the door for the future. I'll need to start tomorrow. What do you think?"

"It's okay with me and sounds like a great opportunity."

After accepting the job, my next call was to the babysitter to see if she was available to help until I made other arrangements. Even though I dreaded the thought of leaving her, I was so relieved that Cindy would be in a safe, familiar setting.

The junior high teaching position was excellent and my department chair was a wonderful mentor. I learned so many valuable teaching techniques from her. I also appreciated the positive atmosphere in the building and having students who responded well to discipline. I especially enjoyed working in tandem with the shop teacher. Together, we designed a four-week program where the girls and boys swapped classes. The guys cooked and sewed, while the girls worked with shop equipment. When the lady on maternity leave didn't return, my part-time position turned into a full-time one that I enjoyed immensely. My career was soaring while my marriage was falling apart.

Cindy and I loved the summer days and the weekends when Bob worked long hours. We both breathed easier when there was no tension and no yelling in the house. She got tired of him ignoring her constantly and learned at a young age to avoid him.

After we moved into the new house, I looked at the newspaper ads for a swing set on sale. Bob always complained about the miles I put on the car, so I thought this was one way to eliminate trips to the park. After he finished his breakfast one morning, I said, "I found a swing set on sale at K-Mart. It's the right price. Cindy needs something to play on."

"No. I don't want the yard torn up with that thing. It isn't necessary."

"But it's a good deal and why is the yard so important? We can't even walk on it because you're so particular about every blade of grass."

He said, "I won't discuss this again!" and stormed out. When he left for work the next day, I drove our big Mercury convertible to the store and bought it. Somehow, the stock boy was able to load it into the car by straddling it across the front and back seats. When we got home, a neighbor helped me put it in the garage.

When Bob got home, he was furious. I'm sure the whole neighborhood heard him. I didn't back down and said, "Listen, this is for your daughter. Why can't you ever put her first? She needs it for her development and entertainment. We can move the swing around on the yard, so it doesn't harm your precious lawn. You're such an expert on everything that it shouldn't take you long to put it together."

Several days later, the swing was in the backyard. It was moved all around and was never anchored down.

Bob and I continued to quarrel, especially when I was off in the summer. Despite my best efforts, I could never please him. After one particularly awful argument, I said, "I'm leaving you for good. I've had it. You don't care about us."

I went to Cindy's room and took her piggy bank from the top of her dresser and packed a bag. We only made it one mile down the road before I pulled into the Gold Circle parking lot. I shut off the engine and wept.

Cindy patted my shoulder and said, "Mommy, you can leave. You don't have to go back."

"Sweetie, I don't have any money and I have nowhere for us to go. I need to make sure you're safe. For now, we need to go back home. Don't be afraid because I'll always protect you."

Bob met us at the door and said, "I'm sorry, honey. I'll make it up to you."

I didn't acknowledge him. It was the same apology I'd heard hundreds of times and nothing ever changed.

Unsettled

We had only lived in our new home three years when Bob said, "Hon, I found a housing development in a suburb that's only 30 minutes away. It's close to my new job. Let's take a look."

"Why are you obsessed with moving all the time? I don't get it. We have a lovely home."

"I don't like our neighbors and it's too far from work."

He eventually wore me down and we built a large Colonial house after he agreed to let me decorate it on my own without having to ask his permission for anything. We moved in early June and I quickly realized what a good decision it had been, especially for Cindy who made friends with the many children on our street.

Shortly after we moved in, Bob was in good spirits and planned a romantic evening, although I didn't think he was capable of feeling that way for long. I had seen this scenario many times and knew what was coming next.

"Annie, I don't like it here. We need to move. I don't have anything in common with the neighbors and I don't like the stairs."

"No. This has to be our last move for several years. This is a great location and a gorgeous home. Cindy starts school in the fall and needs structure and stability in her life. I won't move unless you get a promotion."

He didn't say a word and retreated to his den. I sat down at the kitchen table and bowed my head. *Lord, give me strength to stay with this man. I can't take it much longer.*

By the middle of November, he had become lethargic. When I asked what was wrong, he wouldn't answer. After several minutes of sulking, he said, "I want to move. There are problems at work and I have too much to do."

"I meant it when I said we aren't moving. That's insane."

I dismissed the conversation from my mind and started preparing for Thanksgiving. It turned out to be a wonderful celebration. I enjoyed every minute of hosting it for both of our families. The next day, I was putting things away in the kitchen when I heard the garage door go up. I couldn't imagine why he was home so early. He looked a mess when he sat down at the table and stared at the floor. I waited for him to speak first.

"I lost my job, Annie."

"What? That can't be. You're always telling me that you're the best employee they have. You talked about a possible promotion to district manager. How can the company let you go?"

He didn't respond and the fact that he made no attempt to defend himself baffled me even more. My mind was spinning with questions. I thought about all the late nights when he said he had to go back to the store to shut off the alarm system. I was gullible and believed him. Why was he fired if he was such a trustworthy employee? I needed answers and hoped I would get them from the vice president of his company who was a member of our church.

I went upstairs to check on Cindy and said, "I'll be gone for a little bit but I'll be back soon."

I was shaking when I pulled into the boss's driveway. It was unlike me to be so bold. When he opened the door, I shook his hand and said, "Hello. I'm Bob's wife, Annie. I'm sorry to bother you but he just gave me the shocking news. I don't understand why this has happened. He always tells me that he's a valuable employee. This is worrisome because we just built a new home."

After inviting me to come in and sit down, he said, "Listen, I know this is difficult but Bob did something wrong. Yes, he is a hard worker but this issue cost him his job."

"But what did he do?"

"I'm sorry but that's something he'll have to tell you. I'm sure you're worried about your family's finances but he won't have trouble finding another job. I wish you all the best."

"Thank you. I'm sorry again to have bothered you."

When I walked into the house, Bob was sitting on the stairway step. I calmly said, "Tell me what happened."

"Well, it was a business deal. I got caught doing something wrong. I knew that I'd lose my job if I continued. I'm sorry. Where were you?"

"I went to see your boss."

All the color drained from his face. He stood up and nervously said, "What did he say?"

"He said it was up to you to tell me."

He heaved a great sigh of relief and hurried upstairs.

"I'll make calls tomorrow, Annie. I'll find a new job."

I went into the family room and sat on the sofa. I wondered if I'd ever know the truth. Cindy came over and put her arms around me.

"What's wrong, Mommy?"

"Your dad is looking for another job."

"He changes jobs a lot, doesn't he?"

"He does and I don't know why."

I couldn't sleep that night after such an unsettling day. I not only rehashed everything that had happened but was reminded of something that Bob asked me several months earlier. I didn't think much about it at the time. He read aloud a newspaper article about a man who had been unfaithful to his wife. After finishing, he laughed and said, "Would you leave me if that happened?"

"I would forgive you the first time but if it ever happened again, I would walk away."

A New Life

When my teaching partner and mentor retired, I took her place as the department chair. I was proud of my accomplishment and received many compliments from everyone except Bob, which came as no surprise. Early in our marriage, I saw an alarming pattern of behavior … his jealousy whenever I succeeded at something.

Even though I wanted another child, I never mentioned it. I didn't think he'd agree. That's why I was so surprised one evening when he said, "Let's try for another baby. I want a boy and I've been reading a book that describes what couples should do to determine the sex of their child. I think it has something to do with taking your temperature during ovulation."

I read the book and took my temperature diligently as we tried to conceive a baby boy. After a night of intimacy during the frigid blizzard of 1978, I had a feeling that I'd be pregnant and my intuition proved to be right. I taught until the end of the year and then took a two-year maternity leave.

After my examination on October 5th, the doctor said, "There's a full moon on October 16th and I predict that you'll have your baby on that day instead of your due date on the 23rd."

I laughed and said, "How do you know?"

"I just know the signs."

On the 15th, I couldn't get comfortable and the back pain was so bad that I spent most of the afternoon lying on the floor. My water broke that night and I started having contractions at 10 o'clock. I called my neighbor, Peg, while waiting for Bob to get home. The moment he walked in, I said, "We have to go to the hospital now. The contractions are close."

"But I'm hungry, Annie."

Peg was knocking on our door seconds later, prepared to take me to the hospital if necessary.

"I'm sorry but I'm leaving now with or without you."

I picked up my bag, thanked Peg for staying with Cindy and walked out the door. He followed, grumbling under his breath.

At 12:15 a.m. on the 16th of October, we were blessed with a beautiful little girl. The full moon was shining brightly.

"Bob, we don't have a name picked out. I like Angela."

"No, that's Italian. I like Susan Renee."

"Susan is pretty but it doesn't flow with our last name. What about Suzanne Renee?"

"Yes, I like that. We'll call her Suzy."

"My best friend's name is Suzanne. That's who she'll be named after."

While I loved being a stay-at-home mom, it was exhausting because I received no support. He never got up in the middle of the night to help. While I took care of the girls, fixed dinners from scratch, mowed the yard and took care of the dogs, he did whatever he wanted and golfed every chance he got. In the winter, I shoveled the driveway while he was in his study. I was his live-in maid and he took advantage of it.

He was more attentive to Suzy than he ever had been with Cindy. When I watched him pick her up and hold her, I asked myself why he couldn't have done that with Cindy. As Suzy got older, he read to her and played pitch and catch frequently. Although Cindy handled it well for her age, there were times when she looked at me with a forlorn expression. Consequently, I did my best to think of games that the three of us could play, in order for him to interact with her. She especially enjoyed Parcheesi, so I made a game board with short legs that made it easier for her to participate. When he was in a good mood, it was fun. When he wasn't, he refused to play, no matter how many times she asked.

When my maternity leave ended, I took a job teaching Home Economics at a high school that was only three miles from our home. It didn't take long to get into the routine of getting Suzy to the babysitter's and Cindy to school. Getting back into the teaching routine, however, was more of a challenge. I worked hard finding ways to make my classes appealing to those students who were taking it as an elective. I especially enjoyed being creative in my Adult Life Styles class. One of the highlights was requiring the students to plan and carry out a mock wedding that was held in the auditorium. The project was such a success that it made the newspaper. Bob never said a thing. I wasn't sure if he bothered to read it.

One evening after a terrible argument and a tiring day at school, I opened the liquor cabinet, took out a bottle of rum and poured a generous amount in a glass. I swirled it around, debating whether to drink it slowly or guzzle it and pour another. I had never consumed much alcohol in my life but craved something to numb the emotional pain. I took a small sip and grimaced at the bitter taste, knowing that wasn't the answer. So I got on my knees and asked for help. *Lord, part of me wants to leave him but I don't know where my girls and I would go. I'm lost and need to find my way.*

The tension intensified when Bob came home from work a few days later and said, "Annie, I need to talk."

He was clearly upset, so I said, "Let's sit in the backyard and I'll listen while the girls play."

I expected him to ramble on about his parents or himself. Instead, he said, "I feel so alone."

"How can that be? You have a wife, two daughters, a good job, parents and friends. What is really bothering you?"

"I never made my own decisions. My mother always gave me advice on what I should do with my life."

I hesitated and said, "Did your mother tell you to marry me?"

"Yes. She said you would make the best wife."

My heavy heart sighed in pain.

Symptoms

It got to the point where he just wanted to sit alone and sulk. He barely had enough energy to go to work and often called me from the pharmacy saying, "I don't think I can get through the day."

I was always positive and said, "Yes, you can. You'll be okay."

When conversations with our minister didn't help, I was running out of resources. He took it upon himself to make a doctor's appointment because he feared that he had a serious illness. After a thorough examination, the doctor reassured him that he was fine. Bob refused to believe it and kept saying, "I'm not okay. I hurt everywhere."

In August, I was enrolled to take a post-graduate class. He begged me not to go.

"The kids and I need you at home. I'm too sick. It's selfish if you leave."

"Do you want me to quit my job? I won't be able to keep it if I don't go back to school and pick up extra credentials. Do you want me to retire and take care of the family?"

"Yes. We need you home with us."

After a sleepless night filled with uncertainty, I canceled my class. Nothing was more important than staying home to help our family mend. This meant giving up my job in one of the best school districts. I dreaded having to share this with our assistant superintendent because I knew I'd get emotional. When I walked into her office, I said, "Ms. Davis, I regret having to tell you that I need to resign. It's one of the hardest decisions I've ever made. I know I'm breaking my contract but I have no choice. My husband isn't well and I need to be home."

"Annie, I know you aren't a quitter. You've been a great asset to the district. I wish you and your husband all the best. I am truly sorry to see you go."

My voice cracked when I thanked her for everything.

Unhealthy Attitude

Bob was up early the next morning and was determined to call the doctor again, even though it was a Saturday. I strongly discouraged it but he dialed the number anyhow. Much to my surprise, the doctor answered and said he'd see him. When we got to his office, Bob told me to stay in the car.

"No, I'm going in with you."

As soon as we sat down, the doctor said, "Bob, I have checked everything. I told you last week that you are not ill. If you're dealing with a lot of stress at work, why don't you think about taking a leave of absence until you're feeling better? I'm going to give you the name of a good counselor who has helped other people in situations like yours."

As soon as we got in the car, he said, "Annie, the doctor doesn't understand. I am sick!"

"He's told you more than once that you have no health problems. We're going to follow up with his recommendation of seeing the counselor on one condition. You have to go into it with an open mind."

We were both surprised that he was able to see the counselor so soon. Even though he didn't like answering some of the questions, he was generally in good spirits when I picked him up after each session. There were small visible signs at home that the therapy was helping. He treated me with more respect and made an effort to pay more attention to the girls.

Shortly before I left the house to pick him up from the final session, the phone rang. He was crying and said, "Hey, honey, the therapist won't release me until I confess something to you. I'm afraid you'll leave me after you hear it."

I sensed what he was going to say and cut him off.

"Don't say another word, Bob. Just remember that I have honored my wedding vows throughout our marriage. For better or worse, I have remained faithful to you."

His silence said it all.

Danger

During his recovery, our relationship improved. He was more communicative and affectionate. It was encouraging, especially after learning I was pregnant. But as he became stronger mentally and physically, he returned to his old ways of controlling everything. One of his bizarre demands was telling me that I could only be involved in activities when he was at work.

Whether he liked it or not, I had already made up my mind that I'd help with summer Bible school. I enjoyed my co-workers and loved working with the children. One morning, we were all startled when an ambulance pulled up at a house beside the church. One of the teachers hurried into my room and said, "Annie, please take over for me. I'm going to check on the neighbor."

She returned minutes later and motioned for me to step into the hall.

"He's unconscious after fainting and also cut his head. He's such a nice man. He used to be a member of this church. I'm praying that he'll be okay."

Even though I didn't know him, it was apparent that many in the congregation did when the pastor said in church the following Sunday, "I want to let everyone know that Gene is home recovering from the accident."

My due date was November 25th and when the time drew near, we once again hadn't chosen a girl's name. When I pinned Bob down, he said, "I like Crystal Gwen."

I had no idea where he came up with the name but I wanted to act enthused and said, "I like Crystal but Gwen doesn't work. It would be a mouthful for a little girl."

He thought for a moment and said, "Let's call her Crystal Anne. But I don't know why we're discussing it because it will be a boy."

When I started having contractions, we bantered back and forth whether it was really time to go. As it turned out, we got to the hospital shortly before our third precious daughter was born. After the doctor congratulated us, he said, "The surgery to have your tubes tied is scheduled for 8 o'clock tomorrow morning. I'll see you then."

After I recovered from the procedure, I had so much energy that I volunteered to work on the church recipe book and make costumes for the children's Christmas pageant. When I mentioned this at the dinner table, Bob looked at me with disapproval. I knew an argument was brewing and sent the girls upstairs to play in their rooms.

Without raising my voice, I said, "Okay, so what did I do wrong this time?"

"Why did you volunteer for all of that? You don't have to work on the costumes. I want your time spent on us."

Maybe it was my hormones or maybe I'd finally had enough because I didn't hold back.

"What more am I supposed to do for you? I take care of the kids, clean the house before you get home, cook your meals and do the laundry. You always want everything to be perfect. I'm always here for you but you aren't here for us. All I want is to be part of the church."

I walked to the dining room table and picked up a box of decorated Christmas cookies I'd made earlier. I flung them across the room. The girls came running down the stairs and yelled, "What's wrong, Mommy? What's wrong?"

Suzy started crying and said, "What did you do to the cookies?"

Bob never said a word and went upstairs, while I stared at the mess. When the girls started helping me pick up the crumbled pieces, I told them repeatedly how sorry I was.

A few hours later, he came downstairs and said, "I apologize. I'll try harder."

I was too tired to care.

Tragedy

It started out as a pleasant day on Monday, May 2, 1983, but later turned warm and sticky. It was unusual for that time of year and by late afternoon, a foreboding stillness hung in the air. While holding six-month-old Crystal, I glanced out the window at the ominous sky and dialed the weather station. The recorded message alerted people that a tornado warning had been issued for the area.

"Girls, let's get to the basement. The sky looks scary. It could be a tornado."

At the age of 12, Cindy was such a free spirit and said, "I'm staying on the porch. I want to watch."

"No, it's not safe and I'm not telling you again."

As soon as we were all on the couch in the basement, I turned on the TV. My fear intensified when the weatherman said, "We just received confirmation of a tornado touching down. Stay tuned for further details."

Bob called a few minutes later.

"Annie, are you all okay? Was there any damage?"

"We're fine but there are horrible pictures on TV. It touched down four miles to the east of us. Our church has been hit. The suction from the tornado pulled a wall off its foundation. Worse yet, the house next door to the church is gone."

143

Certain streets were blocked off for several days. When people were eventually allowed to see the devastation, it looked like a bomb exploded. It was heartbreaking to see the single-story house beside the church. The roof had blown off and the family's cherished possessions were dangling from tree limbs and scattered everywhere. Many church members volunteered to look for personal belongings.

"Bob, we should help."

"No. We have to go home. We don't have time."

We soon learned that the wife died when she took shelter behind a dresser in the bedroom. The bricks from the chimney landed on her head and she was killed instantly. If only she had gone into the bathroom that was untouched.

As we got ready for church the following Sunday, Suzy didn't want to go and said, "I'm afraid. I don't want to see the house where the person was killed."

After assuring her it was safe, she finally got in the car, dropped to the floor and didn't look up until we parked. She opened the car door and ran straight ahead to her Sunday school class.

While sitting in church several weeks later, I overheard the man in front of us say to his wife, "Gene is back. He's talking to the pastor in the hall. That's encouraging news."

I turned around just then and saw a tall, distinguished gentleman enter the sanctuary. He smiled and shook hands with everyone. It was obvious how respected he was.

Ultimatum

When Bob's parents came for a visit, I worked hard to prepare a nice meal. They chatted with him and played with the girls in the basement. Just as I was taking things out of the oven, he yelled, "Annie, come down here. I need to talk to you."

"Give me a minute. I'm about done."

When I hurried down the steps and started to tell everyone that dinner was ready, Bob interjected and said, "I need you to go back to work. We can't keep going like this. I can't keep up with our friends. We need additional money."

"Do we really need it? You're the one who wanted me home."

"I didn't tell you to quit. You did that on your own."

"I quit because you couldn't function. Our life was falling apart and you were a mess. I gave up a successful career to help you and to save our family. And now you want me to go back to work? Where exactly?"

I was quiet during dinner and had no desire to converse with Bob or his parents. I felt blindsided. As soon as they left, I said, "Did you ask them for advice about my going back to work?"

"Yes. They're my parents. I always ask them for advice."

"You are married to me, not them!"

When he walked away, Suzy pulled on my pant leg and said, "Mommy, please don't fight tonight."

"No, we won't, sweetie. I'm just upset."

The next day when Suzy was at nursery school and Crystal was down for a nap, I skimmed through the white pages and copied the addresses of suburban and city schools within a 30-minute drive. I then called all 36 and asked for applications. When the rejection letters started piling up, I realized that many school districts weren't hiring Home Economics teachers. When I did have the opportunity for a part-time teaching position, Bob's response was, "No, it's too far. You'd use too much gas. I won't have my car driven that hard."

A few days later, I received a call from an administrator at a city school. When I told Bob that they wanted me to come in for an interview, his comments were even more negative.

"You're not taking my car into the ghetto and have it be stolen or the tires slashed. You will not take that job. Do you hear me?"

"I don't know what you expect then. I gave up the great job I had."

He tossed his dishes into the sink and said, "Start looking through the paper. You'll find something. We need the money."

After spending days scouring the want ads, I noticed an interesting one in Sunday's paper that read: *Person needed to work with a youth program.* I called the next day and asked for an application. After filling out the required information and answering a problem-solving question, I mailed it right away. Two days later, I received a call to report for an interview.

The job was located in the old stockyards building off W. 65th. I remembered the area well, having accompanied a busload of students on a field trip there when I was student teaching. A lot had changed since then, including the elimination of the stockyards. When I walked into the office, a charming lady took me to the interview room where a handful of people were seated. I had no trouble answering their many questions. Even though the job didn't pay that well, it provided the opportunity to teach others and interact with people at OSU.

I had just returned home when the phone rang. It was Mrs. Smith who said, "We were impressed with your interview and are interested in having you join us. You gave good answers and we appreciated your enthusiasm. You have the job if you choose to accept it. You would need to start next week."

I couldn't thank her quickly enough. There were many perks to the 8-5 position, including comp time. I was also looking forward to traveling all over the county for retreats and workshops. One day, my colleague, Connie, and I were the only two at the lunch table. I tried not to change expressions when she told me about her divorce from her demanding husband. I didn't say a word but empathized with everything she shared.

Even though my new job kept me very busy, I still made sure that Bob's dinner was ready when he got home from work. While he ate in front of the TV, I always went upstairs and got ready for the next day. Typically, he left a sink full of dirty dishes sitting in water, despite my asking him to put them in the dishwasher. When I didn't have time to clean up his messes, Cindy did it when she got home from school. Not once did he thank her or show any appreciation.

Before leaving for work one morning, I glanced at my horoscope that read: *Today will be a difficult day; the news will affect your future.* It was dated October 29th.

The day was hectic. After I picked Crystal up on my way home, I played with the girls and prepared dinner. Bob didn't like them to be up when he got home in the evenings, so I tucked them in early. He walked in while I was cleaning up the kitchen. In a cold, matter-of-fact way, he said, "I want a divorce. I want my freedom."

I laughed sarcastically until I realized he was serious. It felt like he was twisting a knife in my heart. I couldn't think of anything to say except, "What did you say? Did we not just work through a difficult time? Did I not just help you get back on your feet? Did we not have another baby?"

"Annie, I'll give you everything … the house, the kids, the money. I just want out."

When he started to explain why he wanted his freedom, I said, "I don't want to hear it. I told you that I would forgive you once but that would be all."

As the days passed, we argued constantly. I couldn't eat or sleep and the girls were affected by the angry chaos. I knew I had to pull myself together for their sake. Typical of his erratic behavior, he came home a few weeks later and said, "I'm sorry. I'm not leaving you."

The following week was even more bizarre when he said, "It's time I buy you a new diamond ring."

I couldn't believe what I was hearing. He said that he still loved me and wanted to stay together. Cindy heard everything and in her mature way said, "Mom, that ring isn't meant for you. Think about it."

I made myself believe that he still cared. Cindy was a young girl. She surely had to be wrong. And yet, I couldn't get her words out of my mind when we walked into the jewelry store.

After dropping Crystal off at the sitter's on Monday morning, I called in sick. I was too upset to go to work. I had a beautiful ring but was still married to a man I didn't understand or trust. I didn't know where to go but it needed to be a place where I could be alone to think and not run into someone I knew. I found myself heading east on the freeway towards the mall.

I walked around aimlessly for hours. I didn't stop, even when my feet ached from walking in high heels. I continually asked God to help me. At one point, I looked around and found myself in front of a bookstore. I couldn't resist going in when I spotted a book on display that was about relationships. After reading the back cover, I felt compelled to buy it. I sat down on a comfortable large sofa in the corner. For the next two hours, I never stopped reading until I finished it.

The last page recommended making a list of the pros and cons of one's relationship. I flipped to the blank page in the back, took out a pencil and made two lists. There were so many cons and only a handful of pros. Seeing it on paper made it real. I knew the girls and I had to leave but I had no idea where we'd go.

I would soon be 40 years old and still felt like I was wandering in the wilderness.

Eyes Opened

The next week, I called our pastor to ask about marriage counseling. I was greatly surprised when Bob said he'd go. While I thought it was a productive first session, he said, "I'm not going back. It's lame. I don't need that stuff."

I continued going on my own and poured out my deepest concerns about our volatile marriage. When the pastor asked questions, I was honest and open with my feelings that had been suppressed for so long ... maybe forever. I admitted how unhappy I was and broke down when describing our many arguments that often turned into yelling matches. I expressed several times how concerned I was that the girls were living in such an unhealthy environment. By the time I was finished, I realized that Bob didn't love me. It was a bold awakening.

At lunch the next day, I said, "Connie, how did you go about getting your divorce? Who was your lawyer and how much did it cost?"

As she explained things in detail, I took careful notes. When she said how affordable it had been, I knew that a divorce was within reach.

When I returned home, I took the girls for a drive and purposely slowed down in front of a large house with a For Rent sign in the yard. I said with certainty, "We'll move into a place like this sometime. It won't be this one but it will be a house where the four of us will live."

The Introduction

A few weeks later, I called a friend from church.

"Helen, please save the front flower bed for me. I'm going to weed it next Saturday. I have a family reunion and can't make the church clean-up day."

"No problem, Annie. Thank you for volunteering your time."

The following Saturday, I fixed breakfast for the girls and explained why I needed to go to the church for a few hours. Cindy was aggravated when I told her that she'd have to watch her sisters while I was gone.

"Come on, Mom. Do I have to?"

"Well, either you help here or come with me to pull weeds."

She walked away and muttered, "Okay, I'll watch them."

When I pulled into the church driveway, the man who lived next door was mowing. Even though we'd never met, we exchanged waves.

I weeded for over an hour. When I sat back and admired how much better things looked, I was startled by an unfamiliar voice who said, "Hello. My name is Gene. I like your work. It looks like you need a break. Would you like to come over for a beer?"

"Yes, thank you. It's nice to meet you, Gene. My name is Annie."

I took off my gloves and when I started to stand, I was stiff from being in one position for so long. He took my arm and helped me up. After I brushed myself off, we walked to his house. With every step I took,

I asked myself if I was doing the right thing. I was concerned how it might look to anyone who noticed.

"Have a seat at the table, Annie. What would you like?"

"I'll have what you're drinking."

"Enjoy it. You have to be tired."

"Actually, I feel pretty good. I do the lawn work at home all the time."

I could feel the tension begin to leave my body. I was so comfortable that I shared I was getting a divorce. I also said that I had never been in another man's house. Gene listened and never interrupted. After I finished, he said, "I'm so surprised. You always look like the perfect family in church."

I laughed and said, "Yes, looks can be deceiving. What about you and your family?"

"My first wife died from cancer and I was left with four children to raise. My second wife died when the tornado destroyed the house. I didn't want to rebuild but it was my only option when no one wanted to buy the land."

"I'm sorry for your losses. I can't imagine enduring so much tragedy. It's getting late and I need to get home to my daughters, Gene. I didn't mean to stay so long."

"I wish you didn't have to go so soon but I understand."

When I pulled in, the girls came running out. Eager to tell on her sisters, Crystal wrapped her arms around my waist and said, "Mommy, we were worried about you. Cindy punched Suzy."

"I didn't mean to be gone so long. Let's go in and have lunch."

I pulled Cindy aside and said, "Thank you for watching them. I met the neighbor who lives beside the church. He invited me in for a cold drink and I lost track of time."

Preparations

I woke up earlier than usual on the morning of June 10th. I was so nervous about my appointment with the lawyer that I didn't know if I could get through it. When the secretary escorted me to his office, I felt calmer after he shook my hand and said, "How can I help? Tell me your story."

An hour later, I had cried my way through every detail of my marriage. I wiped my eyes one final time and said, "I would really like the divorce to be finalized before our anniversary on September 10th. I can't bear to continue living a lie with this man."

"That's no problem as long as the papers are signed on time. You need to tell him immediately that you're divorcing him because he'll be receiving the documents in the next few days."

I walked out of the building and took a deep breath. I had never felt so powerful and free. For the first time, I was finally in charge of my life.

The next day was Bob's birthday. He planned to see his parents and play golf with his dad. I glanced at the kitchen clock that morning and knew I needed to say something before he left. While the girls were playing in the backyard, I opened his study door without knocking. He looked annoyed.

"I have filed for a divorce. You can use the same lawyer. It will be more expensive if you get one of your own."

He sat back in his chair and showed no emotion.

"I think it's a good idea, Annie. The price is right."

"I'm only going to say this once, Bob. If you cause any problems at all, you know that I can make it very difficult for you. So make it easy on yourself. I will fight you to the end if you don't do as the lawyer instructs."

He looked down and said, "I know this is what we should do. We can't go on like this."

"You'll need to sign the legal papers when they arrive next week. Here is the lawyer's card."

I closed his door and when I stepped into the hall, there stood Cindy. She smiled and reached out for a hug.

After he left, I opened the patio screen and told Suzy and Crystal to come in. Once we were all sitting at the kitchen table, I explained the changes that were going to happen. I was careful not to say anything hurtful about their dad.

Crystal looked confused and said, "Mommy, what's a divorce?"

I reassured her that even though her dad and I wouldn't be together anymore, they would still see him but at a different house. Then I went into more detail.

"Girls, we'll have to leave this house but you'll take all your favorite things, your clothes, your furniture and your toys. I don't know where we'll live but I'll find a place."

Suzy was clearly upset and said, "Mom, will I have to leave my friends?"

When I nodded, she ran to her room and cried.

Crystal's eyes opened wide when she said, "Then no more yelling and fighting?"

"No more yelling and fighting, sweetie."

Bob never asked where the girls and I would be going. He was only worried about himself.

"Annie, where will I go? I can't afford a place."

"You can live here until our divorce is final and the house is sold. You can have the bedroom, the master bathroom and the den. I'll sleep with the girls. Let me make this perfectly clear. I won't be your maid any longer. You'll do your own laundry, ironing and cooking. You'll have to keep your area of the house clean when it goes on the market soon."

It was late when I was finally ready for bed. Not wanting to scare Crystal when I crawled in, I gently snuggled up to her. She opened her sleepy eyes and said, "Mommy, why are you in bed with me?"

"Sweetie, I'm going to take turns sleeping with you and Suzy."

Two weeks later, I dropped Crystal and Suzy off at Bible school on my way to work. As I got closer to the church, I could see Gene in his yard talking to several men. I waved as I drove by. On my way out, he was standing alone and motioned for me to stop.

"Annie, how are things going? I haven't been able to stop thinking about you. Listen, if you ever need to talk, please give me a call."

"Thank you. I appreciate that. I have to go or I'll be late."

I smiled all the way to work.

Feelings

I tried to concentrate but kept staring at the phone. After an hour passed, I dialed his number.

"Hello, Gene."

"That was quick," he chuckled.

"You said I should give you a call if I needed to talk."

"I'm glad you did. I'll do whatever I can to help. There is something that I want you to know though. I would have told you the first time we talked but you couldn't stay long. I'm 67. I hope that doesn't scare you because I enjoy spending time with you."

I wanted to say how much I appreciated his honesty but was interrupted by one of my co-workers who walked in.

"I'll have to call you back. I apologize for cutting this conversation short. We'll talk soon."

I couldn't stop thinking about him. Whenever I finished an assignment and was on my way back to the office, I stopped at a telephone booth and called. Our conversations were always short but long enough for him to ask me to come over. As tempting as it was, how could I go to a man's home at night? What would people say? Although we had only been together one time, I missed his company.

One evening after fixing dinner for the girls, Bob came downstairs looking very smug. He threw $30 at me. I didn't make eye contact and said, "What's this for?"

"Why don't you go out and have some fun this evening? You could go to a bar."

"First of all, I find it amusing that you're giving me advice on going out. It's absurd that you think I'd go to a bar to meet a guy. I'd never do that."

Later that night, I called Gene. When he picked up, I said, "It's Annie. I just wanted to hear your voice."

"Why don't you come over? There's nothing wrong with that."

"I want to but I just can't."

Freedom

We talked several more times in the weeks ahead and arranged a long weekend in Columbus during August. Although our time together was cut short when Suzy's softball team won the championship and I needed to get back to watch the playoffs, we had the opportunity to open our hearts to each other.

I knew he loved me but hearing him say the words gave me chills. I touched his face and said, "Gene, I love you too."

He pulled a small box from his pocket. As he slid a lovely ring on my finger, he said, "Annie, I want to marry you as soon as your divorce is final. I don't want to wait any longer."

"I don't either. We'll need to wait a period of time after the decree is finalized. I'll be going to court in early September."

He kissed me gently and said, "I'll talk to the pastor and make arrangements. Let's schedule the wedding for Monday, September 21st. It will be a simple ceremony with just our children, my stepson, and the pastor and his wife. The two of us will go out to dinner afterwards."

"This all sounds perfect. I'm so relieved my house sold quickly but the new owners will be moving in during the first week of September."

"Move in with me as soon as you can. You might as well. I really want to meet the girls. Please bring them over. It's important for them to feel comfortable with me."

"I'll start packing right away. I'll always cherish the memories in the house with my girls but I'm looking forward to spending the rest of my life with you, Gene."

I was both thankful and elated that the divorce proceedings went smoothly. After leaving the judge's chambers, I stepped into the crisp fresh air and felt cleansed of my past.

Bob called out my name in the parking lot. I waited until he walked over.

"Annie, listen to me. This divorce is a mistake."

"No, it's the right decision. I forgive you but you lost my trust. I'm moving on with my life. You can see the girls whenever you aren't busy. The choice is yours. Please leave me alone. I'm done."

When I got home, Gene was there to hold me.

"Sweetheart, are you okay?"

"I am. It's finally over. Our journey together is just beginning. I love you."

I was pleased to see my parents and brother at the table. I appreciated it when Dad said, "You look so happy."

Mom nodded in agreement and added, "We don't know how you lived with him so long."

I was surprised by her comment.

"What choice did I have? You and Dad told me never to ask for help. You said I made my bed and needed to lie in it."

"But we never meant it, Annie."

"Mom, we can't change the past. It's over. We have to move on."

My brother had been silent the entire time. Then he looked at me and said, "I've carried this with me all these years. You know that I was staying at Bob's house the night before you got married. When he came back from the rehearsal dinner, he had a big argument with his mother. He didn't want to go through with the wedding the next day. I'm sorry that I didn't tell you. I was so young and didn't understand what was happening."

"It's okay. It makes everything so much clearer. I'm sorry you had to carry that with you for so long."

Income

Gene and I knew that we would turn a few heads with our 26-year age difference and that's exactly what happened. Some shunned us because it was too hard for them to accept. Those who knew us well, however, recognized how good we were for each other.

Not long after we were married, I knew it was time to start looking for a job. Gene wanted to be generous and provide everything we needed, but I insisted on being as financially independent as possible in taking care of the girls' needs and saving for their college educations. My first step was to follow up on applying for unemployment benefits because my job ended, due to lack of funding. After completing the necessary paperwork, I told the receptionist that I felt guilty about receiving the money.

"Oh, you shouldn't," she replied. "You were laid off and are entitled to this. You lost your job through no fault of your own. Remember, it is only temporary. You will have to report back to us. Here is a card that you'll need to fill out each time you try to find employment."

I scanned the want ads and interviewed for different jobs but wasn't hired for any of them. I was holding out hope that a teaching position would soon be available. Until then, I had no trouble staying busy because there were still many boxes to unpack from the move. While cleaning our bedroom one afternoon, I came across a small bottle of nitroglycerin that I thought was prescribed for heart issues. I immediately thought about a conversation I had with Mom a few months before she and Dad met Gene.

"Annie, how is his health? Does he have any problems?"

"Not that I know of. He's full of energy and seems very fit."

I carried the bottle outside where he was working in the yard.

"Gene, I found this in the dresser when I was putting your clothes away. Why do you have it? What are you not telling me?"

"Do you remember when I was building the addition to the house and I collapsed? The doctors thought I might have had a slight heart problem at the time but it hasn't been an issue. They discovered my blood loss is from bleeding ulcers. I'm fine, Annie."

The Phone Call

In mid-October, I received a call from a school administrator who said, "We'd like to offer you a teaching position. We have openings in three junior highs. If you're interested, you can choose where you'd prefer to go. Would you like to know the different locations?"

"Yes. I'd appreciate that very much."

I wasn't familiar with the first two schools but recognized the third one, having worked in that area with the youth program. I eagerly said, "I'll take the position at the school on Harmon Avenue. Thank you so much. How soon do I start?"

"It won't be until the 1st of November. Please call the building principal, Mr. Roberts, in two weeks and set up an appointment to speak with him."

I found the school without a problem and parked in the visitor lot as instructed. Once I reached the front entrance, I read the directions given to me by the secretary. After I rang the bell, the security guard unlocked the door and let me in. From there, I went to the main office. When I walked up to the counter, no one paid much attention to me, until a lady finally looked up from her desk and said, "May I help you?"

"Yes, I have an appointment with the principal. My name is Mrs. Sauter."

"Welcome. He will be with you in a few minutes. Please take a seat."

She pointed to the chairs lined up along the wall. I sat down beside several students who looked as if they had just been in a fight. As numerous people came in and out, I overheard two teachers talking about the incident. Several minutes later, the secretary said, "Mrs. Sauter, please come this way."

I appreciated the principal's professional demeanor and was very attentive when he said, "It's nice to have you with us. We need you to teach a class called Impact Home Economics to seventh graders. It's designed to meet the needs of inner-city students. You'll teach the standard requirements but you may alter the content in order to best help them. The emphasis should be on developing positive self-esteem in those who have various problems. You'll have no more than 15 students at a time and will teach four classes a day. You'll also be responsible for teaching them how to use the computers in the lab. How do you feel about everything I've described thus far? Are you interested?"

"Yes, I'm very interested. I'm anxious to begin."

My mind was spinning on the way home. I had never touched a computer and knew absolutely nothing about them. After I shared my day with Gene, he said, "I think it's time for you to buy a cell phone. You need to be able to call me if you run into a problem at school or on your way home. I also want you to call me each morning when you get there."

While I appreciated his concern for my safety, I wasn't worried. I just wanted to teach again. I left before 6:30 on the first day to beat the traffic and listened to some of my favorite Christian music on the way. After parking in the garage, I locked the newly purchased club on the steering wheel, pulled the iron gate shut and clicked the lock.

When I walked into the office, some of the staff gave me important tidbits of information. I tried not to act surprised when one of them said, "Your paycheck will be docked if you don't sign in each morning."

Another surprise awaited me when I walked into my room that I shared with a teacher named Brenda. I wasn't sure what I was getting myself into when she said, "Annie, don't be scared when I tell you that you are the third teacher to tackle this job since September. It's only fair that you know."

Since it was only November 1st, I started to wonder just how stressful my classes would be. When the students walked in for homeroom the next morning, only a few responded when I said, "Good morning." The rest walked by me like I didn't exist. After the bell rang, I introduced myself and took attendance. Things were going smoothly until a mouse ran across my feet. Most of the kids screamed and before I knew it, they were all in the hall. The teacher in the next room yelled at them to quiet down, walked them back to the room and said to a student, "Go tell the custodian that we need a mousetrap for room 202."

After homeroom ended, I sat down at my desk to put some papers away. When I opened the drawer, several cockroaches jumped out. I shrieked and slammed it shut. I decided at that point to put things in the storage area. When I unlocked it and flipped on the light, hundreds of them scurried across the floor. I quickly shut the door, just as the teacher across the hall walked in to see how I was getting along.

"Oh, I see you found our friends," she laughed. "I know it really isn't funny. The custodians spray once a month but they come back. Whatever you do, be careful not to take them home with you."

I shook my head and said, "To tell you the truth, I feel like they're crawling all over me."

I learned the hard way when I should or shouldn't intervene with behavior issues. When two boys got into a fight, I tried to break it up and was nearly hit in the head with a chair. The next day, one of my teaching colleagues said, "Here is some advice, Annie. If there is a fight, call for security."

Once the students got to know me and understood what I expected of them, I earned their respect and had very few problems. Wearing suits, dresses and high heels each day set a good example in establishing classroom discipline. I worked hard designing lesson plans that taught them coping skills. When I learned that I had no budget, I spent my own money buying items for various projects. The hardest thing for me to accept was not being able to help every student who struggled. There was only so much I could do.

When I was in high school, aptitude testing showed that I was mechanically inclined. This ability, along with hours and hours of hard work enabled me to become computer literate. When I noticed a computer not being used in another classroom, I asked to have it placed in my room. After I mastered word processing and several other programs, the principal asked me to teach a programming class. The students loved the sessions and voiced their feelings, while I walked around making sure they were staying on task.

One Sunday evening when I was preparing lesson plans at the table, I asked Gene if anything was wrong because he was unusually quiet. He looked up from his recliner and said, "I don't want to alarm you but I've felt strange all day. I'm so tired and short of breath."

I alerted the girls that I was taking him to the emergency room immediately. While I was getting our coats from the closet, they cried and hugged him goodbye. He downplayed how he was feeling and assured them he'd be fine and back home soon.

He was quickly attended to by the medical staff. While we were waiting to hear the test results, I never let go of his hand. I was afraid it was more than a flare-up of his bleeding ulcers. My mind kept returning to the nitroglycerin I found.

It wasn't long until the doctor walked in and said, "Mr. Sauter, you've had a mild heart attack. I'm admitting you to run more tests."

When he was discharged two days later, he was put on heart medication and told to exercise more and change his diet. He was also told to take it easy. On the way home, he said, "Annie, that heart attack isn't going to stop me from living my life like I did before. I have no intention of slowing down."

Defiance

Raising three daughters was challenging at times, especially during Cindy's senior year. She wouldn't listen to me, talked back every chance she got, disregarded her curfew and let her school work slide. I knew Gene was right when he said, "If she doesn't settle down, no good will come of it. She'll be a poor role model for her sisters. You have to put your foot down."

She tested me one too many times when she got home extremely late from a concert one night. When she walked in, I was waiting at the kitchen table.

"Sit down, Cindy, and don't say a word until I'm done. I'm not sure why you're defying me but it's going to stop right now. Your grades have dropped, you purposely antagonize Suzy, your bedroom is always a mess and you refuse to get home on time. There are nights when I don't know where you and your friends are. You have no respect for my rules. If you aren't willing to follow them, you'll have to live somewhere else."

She snapped back, "Fine! I'll leave!"

She went to her room, packed a bag and stormed out. Even though I knew I'd done what was necessary, I couldn't stop the worrisome tears. I hadn't expected her to respond like she did. I felt like a failure as a mother and prayed that she'd realize how good her home life was.

The next evening, Gene and I were playing cards when she walked in and set her bag down.

"I'm sorry for the way I've acted. Please forgive me. I went to Dad's and then to a friend's house. The whole time I was gone, I knew I wanted to be home. I'll settle down, Mom. I promise."

After she hugged us and went to her room, Gene reached over and held my hand. There was no need to say anything. His gesture confirmed what I was feeling. Regardless of the challenges that lay ahead with his children and mine, we'd get through them as a family.

Opportunities

Midway into my second school year, the principal asked me to stop in his office. I had no idea why.

"Mrs. Sauter, I'd like for you to run our new technology room that needs to be operational. Would you be interested in seeing it after school?"

"Yes, I'm very interested."

When he unlocked the large door, I couldn't believe the 42 orange stations that lined the room. I was intrigued when he said, "Each station introduces the student to a career. It is equipped with a TV/VCR, notebook, supplies, and directions that guide the student in carrying out a career investigation. With your excellent management skills, I'm confident things will run smoothly."

"This is a dream come true for me. I've envisioned having a room like this for years. Thank you for thinking of me. I'll need a few weeks to get organized. At a quick glance, it looks like some stations will have to be combined or moved to create more walking space."

"That's fine. Take your time getting it ready. Do whatever you think is best."

My students loved coming to class, especially when I rotated them through the stations that introduced them to different occupations. It was such a success that I was asked to model my techniques to other teachers in the district.

When I returned home each day, Cindy updated me on the newest college she wanted to attend. When she said that her first choice was to go to school in a warmer climate, I shook my head and said, "I wish you could but I can't afford out-of-state tuition. You need to stay in Ohio and Cincinnati is as far south as you can go."

When she was accepted to the University of Cincinnati, I had mixed emotions. We had such a close relationship and I would miss her terribly but I knew it was time to let her go. We were both in tears the day I dropped her off. After an extra long hug, I said, "Please take your studies seriously. It's a must. You're a smart girl and I know you'll succeed. I'm so proud of you."

The moment I drove away, a fresh set of tears appeared. I loved her so much. I always felt bad about the painful moments in her childhood. Somehow, she was able to rise above the adversity and become a strong young woman.

She took my words to heart and made the Dean's list in the first quarter. Even while working part-time, she completed five years of school in four. I was in awe of her drive and determination. Gene and I couldn't have received a more touching Happy Anniversary message than the letter she sent us.

October 6, 1989
Happy Anniversary!

Hi. How are things going? I have something I need to say. I want you to know that I appreciate everything you've done for me. I look back on the past and I can't believe how I acted. No, I don't dwell on it because I would not be here today if that were the case but I want to apologize for all the times I yelled at you. Yes, I will admit I was a little disrespectful but I am sorry. I want to give credit where credit is due. I hope this doesn't sound silly but I've wanted to say it for a while.

Mom, I want you to know how proud I am of you after everything you went through. Tell Gene, Suzy and Crystal that I love them.
I love you, Mom.
Your #1 daughter

Birthplace

I was grateful for the warm welcome my daughters and I received from Gene's family members. We saw his sisters several times a year and enjoyed being with his daughters and their families on holidays and various times throughout the summer. I appreciated their kindness and their sincere efforts to make us feel as if we'd been a part of their family all our lives.

I thanked God daily for Gene. He loved me so much that he was willing to raise a four-year-old, an eight-year-old and a 17-year-old. The girls adored him and often sought his advice as they got older. They blossomed under his guidance and I marveled at his ability to make each one of them feel special. He understood that I needed to be with them as much as possible before they reached that stage in life where they preferred being with their friends. He encouraged me to take them to events and be involved with their school activities. This man of faith never complained about anyone or anything. Whenever someone asked how he was doing, he'd always say, "If I was any better, I couldn't stand it."

After we were married, he suggested that I reconnect with my parents by calling them at least once a week and visiting more often than holidays. Because I hadn't had the freedom to do that in my first marriage, I welcomed the opportunity and so did Mom and Dad. I was elated when Dad reached out and said, "Annie, we're planning a trip to France and would like you to join us, especially since you were born there. This is only my second time going back since the war. There are so many places you need to see." I wanted to go but with all of Cindy's college expenses, I questioned if I should do it, even though I had money from the sale of the house. Ultimately, Gene made the decision for me.

When I mentioned it to him, he said, "You need to go. This is a chance for you to visit your relatives. You've always wanted to do that."

"But I'd be gone three weeks, honey."

"That's no problem. I'll watch the kids while you're gone."

I'm so glad I listened to him. It was an unforgettable trip touring northern France and spending a few days in Paris. I loved seeing my relatives but was disappointed that old age had stolen my grandmother's ability to remember me. I was so moved by Dad's vivid stories. Some of his recollections ended in tears, while others made him smile, especially when he talked about falling in love with Mom. France felt like home to him.

Mom's reactions puzzled me. She acted miserable the entire time. She seemed on guard and was critical of everything. She had a negative response for each positive comment Dad made. When I asked her why she was so unhappy, she said, "Look at the church. It used to be beautiful. No one has kept it up or bothered to paint it. I'm so disappointed in how the cafe looks. My family and I worked hard to keep it nice."

"Mom, I have a favor to ask before we return home. I'd like to see where I was born."

"No, that doesn't matter."

"But it matters to me."

"Don't mention it again, Annie."

There was a mystery in her tone that bothered me. I couldn't help but wonder if she was hiding something from me on purpose.

More Education

On the flight back, I had plenty of time to think about starting my master's degree. Because my pay would increase and I would be a more valuable asset to the district, it was something I needed to do. My only reservations were the tuition expenses and whether or not I was capable of doing the advanced work. Once the coursework was completed, I liked the fact that I could take a three-hour exam instead of writing a thesis.

With Gene's encouragement and others prompting me, I passed the entrance exam at Cleveland State without any problems. The next step was deciding on a major. I considered becoming a guidance counselor but was more interested in pursuing a degree in Computers Uses in Education. Because I knew the work would be demanding, I only took one class a quarter. My life was already overloaded with responsibilities.

The girls enjoyed it when I studied with them at the dining room table. The work was time-consuming but rewarding, which was reflected in my high grades. I was always mindful of expenses and tried to get financial aid, since Cindy was in college. Even though it was disappointing when I was told that I made too much money and was just above the cut-off point, it didn't deter me. I knew I could do it financially if the girls worked while they were in high school and college.

When I got home from class one evening, I saw a letter from Cindy on the kitchen counter. At a quick glance, I realized it wasn't just for me.

I walked into the living room and said, "Gene, this letter is for both of us. Let's read it together."

Dear Mom and Gene,

    I want to tell you thanks for everything! I sometimes take you for granted. Gene, I want you to know how happy I am that you came into our lives. My sisters have the chance to live like young girls and have a terrific father! I don't usually tell you this but I love you. Thanks for treating my Mom with love.

Love,
Cindy

Her words meant so much. They reflected some of the lessons and values that I tried to teach the girls … to appreciate family and to work hard in life. When they asked me to buy them things that I couldn't afford, I said, "If these are things you want, you'll have to get jobs. I also want you to remember how important it is to use good judgment in public. People are always watching and your actions will get back to me. I don't want you to live a sheltered life like I did. I want you to go places with friends and have new experiences but I expect you to act like young ladies at all times."

Gene and I enjoyed our quiet life together. We played cards with friends on the weekends and were active in church activities. I had trouble connecting with the parents of my girls' friends because they couldn't get past how much younger I was than Gene. That was fine. We had each other, our children and a few close church friends. That's what mattered.

Close Call

While attending a district meeting after school one afternoon, I began to feel faint and told the instructor during a break that I needed to leave. Several were concerned about my driving home but I insisted that I could do it. I started doubting my decision when I fought to stay awake and nearly passed out. My body shook when my vision began to fade.

When I walked into the house, Gene gasped.

"Honey, are you okay? You're so pale!"

"My period has been heavier and longer than usual. I need to call the doctor."

I was so weak that my hand shook as I dialed the number. After describing my symptoms to the nurse, she said, "Please stay on the line."

The doctor came to the phone right away.

"Annie, we can do one of three things. You can have another D & C, go on medication or have a hysterectomy tomorrow morning."

"I'll have the surgery. I can't take this any longer."

"Good. In the meantime, get to the hospital right away because you need a blood transfusion."

Everything happened quickly after that. Gene helped me pack a bag and after I hugged the girls goodbye, I said, "Please call Mom and Dad for me."

My blood count was dangerously low and I overheard a technician say that I could have died if I hadn't gotten to the hospital when I did. They continued to pump blood into me all night. Initially, the doctor said I should only be out of work for a week but it took a month to regain my strength.

When I returned to school after spring break, my department chair stopped by to say that the district had decided to turn our building into a computer tech school for elementary students. Those of us who taught there would be relocated to other buildings in the fall. It felt like all of my hard work had been for nothing. I would be moving on but didn't know where.

Instead of dwelling on it, I focused on something positive. Cindy and I were graduating on the same day. Naturally, Gene and I attended her ceremony. There was no doubt in my mind that she would go on to do great things.

Fresh Start

I knew I was in demand as a teacher, having received several verbal offers to go to certain buildings. I turned them all down until I found one that sounded interesting.

"Yes, hello, this is Mr. David and I would like you to join us at our school. I have a tech room that needs to be opened. I know how successful you were at doing this in your previous building."

I liked the strength I heard in his voice and was impressed how well-informed he was about my qualifications.

"Yes, I will take the position."

The following week, I met with him and some staff members. After hearing his vision, I knew I had chosen the right school. My classroom partner, Dianne, and I developed a wonderful working relationship. We received a grant to help students give back to the community. One of the projects was to walk down the street one day a week and serve lunch to the elderly. In spite of being warned that it wasn't a safe area, Dianne and others in our department weren't afraid. Neither were the students. We were continually vigilant of our surroundings and always walked in a group.

I enjoyed my job, although the building was in dismal shape. The bathrooms were dirty and there were gaping holes in the ceiling of the third-floor library that caused water to leak into my classroom storage area. In spite of these negatives, I appreciated the principal's ability to maintain control. We set up a "shirt shop" or dress code to cut down on gang colors and help curtail turf wars. Students were also required to wear dark pants and light shirts with no emblems. When they forgot, they were required to swap their clothes for a dress shirt. The successful teaching strategies that Dianne and I implemented led to exciting speaking opportunities throughout the country.

When I returned from one of our presentations, I was delighted to see a letter from Crystal who had been invited by a friend to go on a family vacation. Even though she was 16, this was a big step for her.

June 21, 1997

Mom,

Hi! How are you? It is 2:20 p.m. We are now on our way to N.C. I've had a good trip. I wish you and the rest of the family could be with me to share in the fun. I just wanted to say thanks for everything you do for me, Mom! I love you! Tell Suzy, Cindy, and Gene I love them too. Talk to you soon.

Love,

Crystal

Connections

I was grading papers when Dad called. He wasn't one to make small talk, so I knew he had something specific on his mind.

"Annie, it's Dad. How are you?"

"I'm doing well. I only have a few more weeks of school left."

"That's why I'm calling. Would Gene mind if you took us to Washington, D.C., for a couple of days in July? Marguerite would like to see the city and tour the Holocaust museum."

"I'd love to go and I know Gene will be in favor of it. The girls can keep themselves busy with activities and work. You'll need some help getting Mom around in her wheelchair. I look forward to the trip, Dad."

Three weeks later, we toured the museum and looked through the archives, hoping to find our cousins' names on one of the lists of concentration camps. When we couldn't locate any information, I was disappointed for Mom. Aunt Colette had contacted the American Red Cross several years before to search for our relatives. For nearly 60 years, the only information we had to go on was that two boys and their Jewish father were trapped inside Nazi-occupied France with nowhere to hide. It was heartbreaking for Mom whenever she thought about her father's sister who she assumed was lost.

She had given up hope and so had I. It felt miraculous several months later when she called and said, "Annie, you will never believe this! They have been found alive. They're living in France!"

I was glad when she handed the phone to Dad because she was talking so fast that I couldn't understand everything she was saying.

"Annie, a lifetime of grief and uncertainty is over. We received a call from the International Red Cross. The officials told us that Daniel is alive and living a few hours from Marguerite's sister. He wasn't the only survivor. His brother, mother and father survived too!"

That ignited a frantic series of calls from my parents' home to New Jersey to Paris to rural Ohio. Mom and her sisters spoke to family members they hadn't been in touch with since 1937. They talked, laughed and cried all at the same time. I had never seen her so happy.

The Party

After seven years at my current school, I was ready for a change. I was exhausted from overcrowded classes. My efforts to keep students in order by constantly changing lessons also proved to be a strain. I quietly submitted my notice to transfer after learning of an opening at a high school on the west side of town. The morning travel would be less stressful and a colleague told me the atmosphere was much better there. I applied for the position and was hired to teach 9th graders. Even though I would be starting all over again in terms of seniority, I knew the change would be refreshing. My only regret was leaving Dianne who had become a close friend.

In January, Gene's daughters and I discussed having a celebration for his 80th birthday. How could we not? He had done so much for all of us. I knew he wouldn't want a fancy party but this was an important milestone. We sent invitations to everyone we knew. Everything was well organized, right down to the caterers, people who wanted to share stories about him, and dignitaries from the community who wanted to attend.

He knew something was up that Saturday morning when I asked him to put on a suit. We walked hand in hand over to the church. The lot was full of cars. It was emotional when we made our way through the crowd to the sanctuary. Crystal put a King's crown on his head and I escorted him to the front where he sat on a chair and faced the crowd. He had trouble keeping his composure, as people shared touching stories about his life and all the good he had done for so many people through the years. I asked those who couldn't attend to send letters that I put in a special binder. It was a wonderful weekend that celebrated a special man. When we returned home that night, he gave me tender kisses of appreciation.

I enjoyed my new teaching position immensely. I loved my students who came from diverse backgrounds from all over the world. Yes, we still had problems with fights in the halls and guns and knives being carried into the building. Most kids, however, came to school because they wanted to learn. My biggest challenge was having 35 students sign up for my class with only 25 computers in the room.

I was so proud and so thankful for my family. Gene was doing well, Suzy was studying abroad, Cindy was working in D.C., and Crystal was in her senior year of high school. I couldn't have asked for more. However, this idyllic time in our lives came to an end on a Sunday evening in October. Gene and I went to bed early and he seemed fine when we kissed goodnight. Minutes later, I screamed, "Crystal, dial 911!"

She ran into our room and said, "What's wrong?"

"It's Gene. He's not breathing. Call 911!"

They arrived immediately. After checking him over, they couldn't find a pulse and pronounced him dead. Seconds later, a young man said, "Wait! I can hear a sound." They continued to work on him in the ambulance and when we arrived at the hospital, he was still breathing.

I sat by his bed all night. He woke up at 7:30 and said, "I love you." He then fell asleep and for several days was in and out of consciousness. Finally, after nine days, he was discharged. I was so traumatized by the scare that I needed counseling.

Unforgettable

On the morning of September 11, 2001, I was presenting a lesson when our department chair came to my room and quietly said, "Annie, please turn on your TV. Something terrible has happened."

The room was eerily silent as we watched the gut-wrenching terrorism. Two planes had flown into the World Trade Center towers and a third one into the Pentagon. There were only smoldering remains of those who died in the fourth plane crash in Pennsylvania. When the bell rang, the students quietly filed out and another class quietly filed in. No one talked. Many parents came to school to get their children.

When I arrived home, Suzy was talking on the phone to Mom. She was in tears and said, "How did you do it, Grandma? How did you go on during the war?"

I put my arm around her and heard Mom say, "You must stand firm against the enemy. You have to pick up the pieces and keep moving on. You can't stop."

The following spring, Gene had a pacemaker and defibrillator put in. While he was trying to adjust to these devices, the recurrent GI bleeds of unknown origins also took a toll on his body. His back pain was so bad that he doubled over in pain one Sunday in church. We rushed to the hospital where a CT scan of his abdomen revealed a 7 cm aortic aneurysm connected to the renal arteries.

The ER doctor talked to me privately and said, "I can get you into the Cleveland Clinic in 10 minutes."

"Do it!" I said.

Prior to surgery the next morning, the doctor said, "Mrs. Sauter, your husband may not survive this or he could end up being incontinent. It's a precarious situation."

I nodded that I understood.

Although he was weak from having lost so much blood, he was discharged several days later. He refused to let it get him down, in spite of the doctor saying it would be a long recovery. We were planning Suzy's wedding and he was looking forward to walking her down the aisle, along with her father. I was concerned if he'd be able to do it because of numerous blood transfusions but there was no doubt in his mind. He was determined to keep his word.

Adapting

As Gene's health declined, his doctor was adamant that he avoid strenuous activity, which included mowing the lawn, trimming the bushes and gardening. When I arrived home one afternoon, he was using the hedge trimmers with his arms extended above his head. I couldn't believe it.

"Gene, what are you thinking? The surgeon said you can't do this kind of thing any longer. You're putting your heart in jeopardy. I know you don't like hearing it but we'll find someone to do the work."

The following Sunday, I pulled the Homes section out of the newspaper. I knew it was time to find another house to make it easier for both of us. I saw one that I liked and was pleased that it was in our price range.

After showing Gene the picture and information, he said, "Hon, if you think we need to move, it's okay with me."

"Do you want to go with me?"

"No, you can look. I trust your judgment."

So I called Suzy and said, "How would you like to look at new houses with me?"

After an extensive search, I settled on a model in a community that was in another county. I wanted to stay local but the prices were too high and most of them had a second floor. The only negative was being half an hour from where we lived. I made up my mind, though, that I wouldn't let the distance interfere with our routines. We drove to church and I took

Gene to Kiwanis every Monday. We also continued to play cards with our friends on weekends. I was pleased with our new home and looked forward to spending a lot of time in it after I retired. It was still hard to believe that we no longer had to mow the yard and shovel snow.

A Difference

It was now 2004 and the last year of my teaching career. In some ways, I wasn't ready to retire but knew I should. The new superintendent insisted that all students be prepared for college and I didn't agree with his philosophy. A lot of students weren't college material. Many were eager to learn a trade and work with their hands. I related to that. I also wondered if some of us would be able to keep our jobs another year, as vocational programs were typically the first ones to be cut in the budget. This was hard for me to accept, having spent so many years promoting them.

I had 39 students assigned to two of my classes and only had 33 chairs. When I left the building at the end of the day, the room temperature was 94 degrees. I had run four fans all day which helped very little. The following week, three more students were added to my roster. On top of that, it was only September. I was burned out and submitted my resignation with no regret.

When I started sorting papers and packing up things in my room, I found a letter I had saved.

Dear Mrs. Sauter,

Thank you for the clothes you gave me. God should bless you. My whole family said you must love me and I told them how much I love you. When I was in your room, I didn't get into fights. I listened to you and did the work. I love you with all my heart. It's the truth. You are like a mother to me. When I first met you, I knew you were special!

Yours truly,

Nora

It was rewarding to know that I made a difference in a student's life. I would miss those moments.

Sorrow

I began to adjust to the new lifestyle of caring for Gene. I missed the interaction with my teaching colleagues and students but not the lesson planning, paperwork and discipline problems. I found new avenues to stay busy. I helped neighbors whenever I could, joined another canasta group, continued with Bible study and helped out at church.

Gene had been in and out of the hospital many times in the past four years. We were at the Cleveland Clinic once or twice a week. Although he wasn't in any pain, he had many health problems that included high blood pressure. I took it often and kept a daily journal. The trips to see his daughters were now out of the question and he no longer went with me to Buffalo. The winter snowbird trip to Florida was canceled and we stopped planning the trip to Alaska. The doctor made sure he had Gene's complete attention when he said, "Mr. Sauter, you have too many serious issues to go too far from home."

In late October, Crystal and I traveled to Buffalo to spend a weekend with Cindy and her family. I was so homesick to see my grandchildren. Because I wasn't comfortable leaving Gene alone, his nephew came to stay with him. I had a busy day with everyone on Saturday and didn't call to check on him until later in the evening. I was surprised that he wasn't home at 9 o'clock. I knew something was wrong and continued to call until I finally reached him at 10:30.

189

"Hey, sweetheart, how are you? I hope everything is okay. I was worried when you didn't answer my calls earlier."

"Hon, we just got back from the hospital. Scott had a massive heart attack today. He isn't expected to live. I'm struggling to accept it. He's only 53."

"I'm so sorry, Gene. We'll leave now and I'll be home soon. I love you."

Crystal and I threw our clothes into suitcases and arrived in Ohio at 4 o'clock in the morning. I stayed by Gene's side as he grieved. The following day, the doctor said, "There is no brain activity, Mr. Sauter. Your son will never get better."

We talked privately and Gene made the decision to let him go. He walked into the hall when the nurses came in. He couldn't bear watching. I appreciated our pastor being with Crystal and me when the machines were turned off.

We were walking around in a daze when Gene picked out the casket and made other decisions for the funeral. It was heart-wrenching to watch him prepare to lay his son to rest. On the way home, he said, "Annie, when we get back, I'm going to call the funeral home and make an appointment to prepay my funeral. I don't want you to have to deal with this the day it happens."

It was hard to put everything in perspective. Crystal and I had gone away for a bit of fun and came home to a tragedy. I could do nothing more than put my arms around the man I cherished.

Warning

May 16, 2006

Dear Mr. Sauter,

It was a pleasure to see you at the recent clinic visit. I have received your test results, which show that there has been deterioration in your kidney function. Please be sure to keep your appointment with the nephrologist later this month.

Sincerely,

Dr. David

I put the letter down and thought of the conversation that Gene had with his doctor a year earlier. He was unwavering when he said, "I don't want to go through dialysis. I knew someone who did and I'm not interested."

The doctor said, "You have the right to decide but you should discuss it with your family first."

"No. The decision is made."

"Gene, without treatment, you may live anywhere from one week to several months. The length of time depends on the amount of kidney function left and your overall medical condition. As the toxic wastes and fluid build up in the body, you may feel more tired and it will be more difficult to breathe."

We were soon staring at the sterile walls in the nephrologist's office. Gene said very little. When the young doctor walked in, he introduced himself, looked at me and said, "Are you his daughter?"

"No, I'm his wife."

He nodded and sat down on a stool.

"With all of your health problems, someone is surely watching over you, Mr. Sauter."

"Yes, God has been good to me."

"The tests indicate that you are now in stage 5 of renal failure. One kidney has failed and the other is operating at 20 percent capacity."

He placed his hand on Gene's knee and said, "The next step is hospice care. You refused dialysis treatment last year when you entered stage 4. I know this was your personal choice. Mr. and Mrs. Sauter, do you have any questions?"

I didn't know what to say after hearing the grim news. I couldn't imagine how I'd live without him. What questions do you ask when your loved one has been given a death sentence? Only God knew the answers.

Later that day, we went for a long ride because I knew the hospice team would be there when we got back. He loved listening to music, so I played one of our favorite CDs. I felt a chill when I heard the words: *At last, my love has come along.* I looked over and said, "This is our song, Gene."

He smiled and said, "Do you see all the trucks? There are more and more on the road."

There weren't more but his double vision made it appear that way.

He showed little emotion after meeting the hospice worker. When she asked him if he had any questions, he coherently said, "When will the defibrillator be shut off?"

I could barely breathe when she said, "It would be wise for you to make an appointment. You need to call while you're thinking clearly and can make your own decisions. This way, it doesn't rest on the shoulders of the family members. If the defibrillator stays on and you start the final phase, it will go off and continually shock you."

His hand felt warm against mine when he said, "Let's make the appointment."

After the worker left, he grinned when I said, "Let's go get a banana split."

He didn't need to watch his diet any longer and I wasn't going to deny him anything that sounded good. As we got closer to the Dairy Queen, he said, "I don't think I can eat one. A vanilla cone will do."

After we got home, I helped him settle back in his chair and said, "I need to get your prescription. I'll be home soon."

My heart sank when he looked up and said, "I love you lots."

"Love you too. See you in a few minutes."

After picking up the medication, I headed towards the exit. My mind was preoccupied and instead of looking both ways, I turned down a side street and was sideswiped by a dark green vehicle that I never saw coming. I immediately got out to check on the elderly ladies and apologized profusely. Fortunately, they weren't hurt. The police officer arrived quickly and after giving him my pertinent information, he asked me to pull into the parking lot across the street. I called Gene right away and assured him that no one was injured. I was cited for failure to yield. I knew this had to be a sign to slow down and be more aware of the present. I thanked God for the wake-up call.

The next day, I walked back to the bedroom to check on him.

"Honey, do you feel up to playing cards tonight? You've been asleep for hours."

"Yes, that sounds good."

I stood beside him while he got ready. I was glad that he still wanted to play pinochle with his close friends. He had started the group nearly 19 years ago after we were married. When he was ready, he asked for his cane instead of the walker. With help, he made it into the house and to the card table. Even though he and his partner never won a game, they had fun. As the evening came to a close, I asked if he needed to use the bathroom before we left. When he said he didn't, I whispered, "Are you sure?" He nodded his head.

As I pulled into the garage, he was in a hurry to get out and nearly opened the door before I stopped.

"Gene, please wait until I come around to help you."

Once inside, he was in a hurry to take off his jacket. When I was hanging it up, he walked out of the laundry room with his cane in hand. He was only six feet ahead of me when he collapsed and landed on his back. I couldn't do anything but scream when his head hit the wooden blanket rack behind the sofa.

I dropped to my knees and saw the vacant look in his eyes before they closed. Once I was sure he was still breathing, I crawled to the table and reached for the phone to call hospice. The lady who answered asked me repeatedly to calm down. When I was able to tell her what happened, she said, "It will be several minutes before we can call you back with more information. Please keep him comfortable until then."

I cradled his head in my lap and covered him with a blanket. He was motionless and pale. For the next several minutes, I prayed and repeated how much I loved him. Suddenly, he opened his eyes. I pleaded with him to lie still but he was determined to crawl to the sofa and try to stand. I begged him not to move, while I ran to get his walker. From there, he let me help him to the bathroom and to bed.

"You have to listen to me, Gene. You can't get up. I need to unlock the front door and turn on the outside light for the nurse."

She arrived a few minutes later and after a thorough exam, she said, "His blood pressure is elevated but he hasn't broken any bones."

She then looked at him and said, "Who is the woman standing beside me?"

"Annie, my wife."

"Gene, do you recall what you were doing earlier this evening?"

He couldn't remember until she gave him a hint.

"That's right," he said. "I was playing cards."

When he didn't remember falling, she took me aside and said, "I think Gene had a mild stroke."

Ready

The next day was a blur. While Gene watched TV, I called his daughters and my girls to tell them about his fall. They were all extremely concerned and wanted me to keep them updated. When I sat down to watch the OSU game with him, it was only 7 o'clock. The first quarter was just ending when he said, "Hon, I'm ready for bed."

The following morning, I helped him get dressed as we prepared for a visit from Carol, the hospice social worker. After I explained to her the details of his fall, she looked at him in a caring way and said, "Are you ready?"

"Yes, I am."

Her question and his answer stunned me. I wanted to cry. It felt as if she knew exactly how many days he would live. As she got ready to leave, she shook his hand and said, "It has been a pleasure to know you, Mr. Sauter."

He smiled.

I walked with her to the door and quietly said, "How will I know? I'm so nervous. What will happen?"

She put her arm around me and said, "It will just happen."

When I woke up the next morning, I was startled by the pungent odor of urine. I immediately laid my hand on his chest to make sure he was breathing. He seemed to be comfortable, so I got dressed and slipped out to the kitchen for a cup of coffee. I checked on him several times until he was awake and ready to get up.

"Gene, do you want to go to the bathroom?"

"No, but I'm hungry."

He stared at the TV while I fixed him some toast. It was alarming when he picked up the whole slice and tried to cram it into his mouth. He was unable to chew and seemed disoriented, so I broke it into tiny pieces that fell on the plate. With tears tumbling down my face, I put my arms around him and said, "It's okay. Let's get you back in bed."

I helped him up from the chair and we slowly made our way back to the bedroom with my arm around his 5'10" frame. He rested until noon and said, "I'm hungry." After helping him to the table again, he took a few bites of stew and wanted to go back to bed. When I covered him up, he started talking gibberish.

I laid my fingertips on his lips.

"Please close your eyes and rest. I'll be back."

A hospice volunteer immediately answered my call.

"Hello. How can we help you?"

I was crying so hard that I stumbled over my words. "C-Can you send a nurse?"

"Yes. We'll send one right away."

I sat on his side of the bed as the gibberish continued. At one point, he said, "Hazel, I love you."

After the nurse examined him, we walked into the hallway.

"Mrs. Sauter, his system is shutting down. His kidney function has stopped."

I knew what she said but couldn't process it. She asked me more than once if I needed help.

"I'll be okay," I said with skepticism.

She reached for my hand and said, "Call us if you need assistance."

"Thank you. Please leave the door unlocked when you leave."

I watched him sleep fitfully. He woke up several times, never once calling me by name. I was now Hazel. At one point, he wanted to get out of bed and tried to remove his Depends. I could see the anguish in his eyes when he lost control of his bowels. I tried to clean him up but couldn't lift his body.

"Oh, God, I can't do this."

I reached for the phone and called hospice again. I felt like a failure. Through the tears, I stammered, "This is Annie. I can't do this ... he needs more help ... I can't go on."

"Don't worry. An ambulance will be there shortly."

It arrived sooner than I anticipated. When the men pushed the stretcher down the hall, the sound echoed as they got closer to our bedroom. I appreciated how gentle they were with him. When the nurse walked in, I rose to greet her but fell apart in her arms. She held me with compassion when I cried, "I'm sorry. I'm not strong enough. I'm not what he needs."

"You've done enough. Now it's our turn to take care of him. We have the pain meds he needs. He won't suffer. Please come with us."

I kissed his forehead after they put him on the stretcher and watched as they wheeled him out the front door and loaded him in the ambulance. I went back into the house, picked up my keys and headed to the garage.

Sometime during the day, I made calls to Gene's family, my girls and close friends. Suzy, Crystal, Brian and Joe stayed with me for several hours. When Cindy arrived, she and I spent the night by his side and were together the next day when visitors stopped in. It meant so much to have our pastor with us.

When the nurse came in to check on him, she said, "His skin has changed. Notice how his legs are blotchy and purplish. The mottling is slowly working its way up."

I looked over at Cindy. She was exhausted like all the rest of us.

"Sweetie, tomorrow is your birthday. You need to be with your family."

"I'm torn. I miss my kids but I'm afraid to leave, Mom."

"Gene would want you to be home."

Tears rolled when she leaned in and said goodbye to him.

"Gene, I have to take care of the boys. I know you understand. I'll see you soon. Love you."

After a tearful hug, I said, "Be safe, honey. I love you. Let me know when you get home."

Later in the day, the nurse returned to examine him and said, "I can't believe this. His skin looks far more normal. The mottling has disappeared from his legs. He's holding on and isn't ready to go."

"It's my daughter's birthday today. He must have heard us discussing it last night. I don't believe he'll pass today."

The nurse nodded and said, "Yes, they can still hear you and they do comprehend."

As the day progressed, his skin continued to look healthier and was cool to the touch. When I tucked him in that night, I covered his body with a warm blanket. I kissed him goodnight and said, "Thank you, my love, for not leaving today. You are a wonderful man. I never knew that love could be so deep and tender until I met you."

I sat there until midnight and then crawled into the bed that had been pushed up against his. I was afraid he might pass and I wouldn't be there. I turned towards him and touched his face. How I wished I could be in his arms once more.

I lay in the dark thinking about something special I could give to my girls that was connected to Gene ... mementos that would always be a reminder of this man they loved dearly. I had already created photo albums for family members in the summer but I wanted to do more. I knew that I'd give Cindy the ring he gave me on our 10th wedding anniversary and Suzy would get the necklace he bought me on our 5th anniversary. I struggled in knowing what to give Crystal who wanted him to walk her down the aisle. The answer came to me when I laid my hand on top of his and touched his wedding band. I knew then that I would give her the ring for Joe to wear on their wedding day. It was so important to me that Gene would be with them in spirit.

At 4:45 in the morning, he began to gurgle. It was a sound I hadn't heard before. I rolled closer to him and stroked his face, head and arms. I believed then and will always believe that he heard me say, "Gene, my dear, it is okay to go. Please rest in peace. Thank you for the love you have given to all of us. I love you."

I prayed silently and then said aloud, "Dear Jesus, I roll him over to you. Please take him in your arms ... not my will but thy will be done."

As I said the Lord's Prayer, his breathing became shallow. Then there was only silence. I moved my hand to the front of his mouth and felt no air. It was over. He was with the Lord.

I sat up, gently put my feet on the ground and reached over to kiss him on the lips. I crossed the hall to the nurses' station and said, "Mr. Sauter passed at 5:33."

The nurse who was standing next to me said, "Please sit in the waiting room until we finish, Mrs. Sauter. We'll come and get you so that you can wait with your husband until the ambulance arrives."

Several minutes later, I returned to the room. Gene's body was draped with a white sheet pulled up to his chin. He had a smile on his face. I laid my hand on his cheek and talked to him until he was transported to the funeral home.

I had called one of the girls while I waited and they all arrived in time to say goodbye. I was shocked to see Cindy who should have been in Buffalo.

"Mom, the craziest thing happened. As I approached Erie, I drove into a blinding snowstorm that wasn't predicted. There was zero visibility, so I had to turn around and come back. I spent the night with Suzy."

We said our goodbyes to the staff and thanked them for taking such excellent care of Gene. We followed the men out of the building and watched as they wheeled him into the hearse. After we cried and hugged each other, I realized we hadn't eaten much in the past few days. I said, "Let's go to Bob Evans. It was Gene's favorite restaurant."

When we walked in, I said, "Table for seven." The young girl took us to a round table in the corner of the room and passed out the menus. She returned minutes later and said, "I was waiting for the other person to join you. When do you expect him?"

We looked at the empty chair beside me. My arm was around the back of it.

"No, he won't be joining us. He passed away this morning. I missed the count."

"I'm sorry," she replied.

We tried to eat but just picked at our food. When the waitress passed by, I said, "We're ready to leave. May I have the tab?"

"Oh, breakfast is on us. We are truly sorry for your loss. Gene was a wonderful man."

The kind gesture evoked more tears.

The wake was Monday afternoon and evening with a short break in the middle. I welcomed the opportunity to sit down briefly. Suzy walked over and said, "Mom, you will never believe this. Bob Barker retired from *The Price is Right* today."

I couldn't help but smile. The girls knew if Gene was watching that show, he was busy. Shortly after we met and began talking on the phone, he often had it on. He enjoyed it so much that he planned his mornings around it. What a coincidence that they both left at the same time. Gene would have gotten a good laugh out of it. For the viewing, I put a box of playing cards by his side, a Kiwanis pin and cross on his lapel and the newspaper article about Bob Barker by his hand.

The funeral service at the church was beautiful and so befitting of such a great man. As the procession approached the gate to the cemetery, I felt his presence when an eagle soared above.

Carnations

I knew what people meant when they said, "Annie, it just hasn't registered yet."

Each room was filled with Gene's scent. At one point, I thought I saw him turn the corner and go into our bedroom. I looked at the paperwork and packages piled on the table and ignored everything. I walked down the hall crying, "What am I going to do without you?"

I was so exhausted that I fell asleep on the hallway floor by our bedroom. I was sore when I woke up and wasn't thinking clearly when I climbed into bed fully clothed. Nothing changed the following day. I was staring into space when the phone rang.

"Hello."

"Annie, it's Dad. How are you?"

"I'm okay."

"We're sorry we couldn't be there for the funeral but your mother isn't well. We don't know what's wrong."

"Dad, I understand. I'll be down tomorrow. I need a day..."

"Good. We'll see you tomorrow. Love you."

I picked up a pen, sorted through the paperwork and began the process of writing thank you notes and notifying companies of Gene's death.

It was sprinkling when I started out the next day. I couldn't help but notice that the landscape had changed. November had descended everywhere and the stark trees added to my loneliness. Normally, I listened to the radio or played a CD but I couldn't bear hearing any music that might trigger a memory. As I approached the exit, I decided to stop at a small floral shop and buy a bouquet of carnations for Mom.

The bell above the door jingled as I stepped into the fragrance of fresh flowers. Before placing my order, I looked at the statues, baskets and memorial stones that lined the floor. A gentleman popped his head around the corner and said, "May I help you?"

"Yes. I'd like a dozen carnations, all colors, and please add baby's breath and other greenery to the bouquet. Thank you."

While I waited, I noticed several plaques on a shelf that were about eight inches high. After reading the many inscriptions that dealt with loss and grief, I was particularly drawn to one that captured what I was feeling … an emptiness without Gene that left a void in my heart.

When my order was ready, I wiped away a few tears and said, "Sir, I'll also take this. My husband just passed away."

He looked at me over the rim of his glasses.

"I'm sorry for your loss. I just set those out before you walked in."

Bittersweet

Mom was on the sofa when I arrived. While the swelling in her face had gone down a bit since the last time I saw her, she was clearly in poor health. When she insisted that her cough was better, Dad shook his head.

After lunch, I shared the details of the past week. When I finished, Mom said, "Annie, I want you to know that Gene said he loved me the last time I saw him. I was moved by his comment."

"I'm sure he meant it, Mom. His kindness was genuine."

A torrent of tears was building inside me and to avoid falling apart in front of them, I said, "I'll go to the drugstore and get you some cough medicine to help clear the congestion."

When I returned, she asked me to clean out the refrigerator and wipe down the kitchen cupboards. I was glad to do it. Staying busy was a good diversion. The next day, I felt much better seeing her dressed. I kissed them goodbye at 5 o'clock and said, "I'll be back. Find things for me to do."

I cried the entire way home. When I walked into the kitchen, the phone rang. It was Bert.

"Hey, Annie, we're playing pinochle next week. I hope you can make it. We'll have the group for dinner from now on when we play cards here, so please come an hour earlier. You don't need to bring anything. Oh, by the way, our friend, John, will be here. His wife passed away in August of 2004."

I listened but really didn't pay attention to anything he said. When he finished, I politely said, "Thank you for the invitation. I'll be there. See you soon."

I enjoyed the people in the card group and looked forward to dinner. I was tired of restaurant food and nibbling on vegetables. As I got closer to Bert's house, my nerves were getting away from me. How could I walk in without Gene? How could I keep from crying? How could it not be bittersweet, knowing that he had played cards with his friends only a month earlier? When I knocked on the door, my throat started to tighten.

All eyes were on me when I walked into the room. I quickly said, "Sorry I'm late. There was a lot of traffic."

I continued to talk nervously with everyone and noticed a stranger across the room. I assumed it must be John. We glanced at each other and looked away.

Lost

Each time I listened to Gene's voice on the answering machine, I was overwhelmed with memories. I couldn't even find the strength to watch the DVD from the funeral service. As crucial as church was in my life, I avoided it too. I hadn't been there for six weeks and nearly talked myself into staying home again but knew I needed to go because Crystal and Suzy were expecting me. I woke up that morning feeling weaker than usual and barely had the energy to bend over the sink and wash my hair. I was so tired that I dreaded the 25-mile drive.

I promised myself that I wouldn't get emotional but when I pulled into the parking lot, tears started gathering when I saw the house next door. I thought of that day in June and envisioned him cutting the lawn. Since the church renovations, the front flower bed was gone but I remembered every detail about the day we met.

I was running a little late and wasn't surprised when my cell phone rang. It was Crystal.

"Mom, where are you?"

"I just pulled into a parking spot. I'll be right there."

I shut off my phone and waved to Suzy as she drove by on the way to the back parking lot.

We all hugged and entered through the back door. The service had already begun and others were in the pew where we always sat. After being ushered to a section across the aisle, Crystal said quietly, "Do you want to eat lunch at the Red Lobster after church?"

"Oh, no, I can't go. I know Gene loved that restaurant but thanks for asking, honey."

My head was throbbing and my eyes were stinging with tears when I went forward for Communion. I could barely see the pastor as I took the wafer from his hand. I left the sanctuary as soon as the service ended. I couldn't get out of there fast enough.

Crystal motioned for me to get in her car and said, "Mom, come with me." We soon joined Suzy at Eddie's Creekside for lunch, which gave me the opportunity to be honest with them.

"Girls, I'm not sure I can go back to church without Gene."

Crystal responded with a sympathetic look and said, "You don't have to make a decision yet. Take your time."

When we finished, Suzy drove me back to the church to pick up my car and asked me to meet her at the mall. After she did some quick shopping, she said, "Mom, I have one more stop. I need to pick up a card."

I waited for her outside of the store. Minutes later, she pulled something out of the bag and said, "I'm going to give these to all of you this year."

She handed me an ornament inscribed with these words: *I love you all dearly, now don't shed a tear, I am spending Christmas with Jesus this year.*

I gave her a hug and kiss as we said goodbye. I didn't have the heart to tell her that I might not put up a tree.

Decline

I had never been without someone, whether it was my parents, first husband, children or Gene. I had reached a point with my grieving, though, where my girls were worried about me. It felt like an unfair burden to put on them and I knew that I was the only one who could do anything about it.

While walking around the block on an unseasonably nice day in January, my neighbor spotted me and said, "Annie, how would you like to see Alaska? Let's go on a cruise in August."

"Sure. Go ahead and plan it and let me know what you find out."

Even though it had been a spontaneous decision, it was the right one. I loved to travel and Gene and I had talked about going there. It was the only state he hadn't visited. My girls were delighted but quickly added, "Save some time on your calendar for us. We're glad you go to the farm every week but we miss seeing you."

I understood their sentiments but they had jobs, significant others and friends to lean on. It was different for me. The farm had always been my refuge and the one constant in my ever-changing life.

I needed to be with Mom and Dad as much as possible. She seemed worse each time I visited and she was becoming increasingly unsteady on her feet which led to a fall. Thankfully, she didn't break anything but caring for her was becoming too much for Dad. That's why I was hesitant when he asked me to take them to New Jersey to visit Aunt Colette. I didn't think Mom was physically up to the 12-hour drive but she was determined to go, so we started out at the end of January.

She sat in the back and said very little, while drifting in and out of sleep. Whenever she complained about having trouble breathing, Dad told her to use her inhaler. When I suggested staying overnight somewhere, he wouldn't hear of it. After several hours of driving, I insisted on stopping at a rest area. When I told Mom I'd help her, she said she didn't have to go. I found that hard to believe since she was taking water pills.

Dad said bluntly, "Did you take all your medicine?"

"No. I didn't bring my water pills. I could have never handled this trip if I did. It's too difficult to get to the bathroom."

A few hours later, Cindy called and we had a lengthy conversation. She needed to vent about something and I was glad to listen. When we finished, I started to share what we talked about but I didn't get very far. Mom firmly said, "You are too involved in your daughters' lives. Let them solve their own problems. It will be good for them."

I was offended by her comment but didn't say anything. If I had, I would have said, "I'm always here for my girls. I wish someone had been there for me."

I drove in silence the rest of the trip, other than bantering back and forth with Dad who insisted he had a better sense of direction than the GPS. By the time we reached Aunt Colette's, I was exhausted. As soon as I stopped the car, Mom needed to use the bathroom. I knew she didn't feel well because she was reserved and not her usual bubbly self with her sister.

The next morning, Dad was agitated when he walked into the kitchen and said, "Your mom wants to go back home. She can't get warm and is having trouble breathing. She didn't sleep well last night and wants to leave as soon as she gets dressed."

There was little conversation during the drive home. She was wrapped in a blanket and the heater was on high. I thought my head would explode.

209

Each time I asked if she wanted to stop at a rest area, she said, "No, I'm okay. I put on a pair of Depends. Just keep going."

When I insisted that we pull off for lunch, she wanted to stay in the car. After a heated argument in French, Dad demanded that she get out, eat and go to the bathroom.

By the time we got home, there was a strong odor of urine in the car. When she apologized for the back seat that was soaked, Dad assured her it wasn't a problem and he would get it cleaned. Once we got her in the house, he said, "I'll take her to the doctor tomorrow, Annie."

The Release

One of the best decisions I ever made was joining a bereavement group after Gene's death. Although I hadn't yet shared my story, I felt safe with everyone who had also suffered great loss. I appreciated the fact that no one ever passed judgment. Towards the end of one of the sessions, I opened up with details of my life that I had never before verbalized.

I took a deep breath and said, "I'd like to thank all of you for making me feel so comfortable. I'm ready to let go of feelings I've buried since my childhood. As a little girl, I didn't have the freedom to say what I thought. I was often punished by my dad for reasons I didn't understand. As a young man, he fought on the front lines and when he returned home, he was hardened to the point that my mother and his parents didn't recognize him. What I didn't realize at the time is that he was suffering from PTSD. He worked nonstop as a way of covering up the haunting memories of war. I couldn't do anything right in his eyes and this led to me growing up with anxiety, fear and no self-confidence. I felt invisible around him. Sadly, I thought this was how other families lived. When I was a young adult, I walked away from that environment and married a man who I thought would make my dreams come true. I was so naive. After much heartache, I couldn't take it any longer and filed for divorce. I had to for the sake of my daughters. I've always felt especially bad that my oldest daughter, Cindy, had to witness so much as a young girl. By the grace of God, I met Gene Sauter. He loved me and my girls with his whole heart. They adored him. He was kind and trusting and encouraged me to become an independent thinker. In a sense, I was reborn after I met him and discovered an inner strength that I never knew existed. I learned that I didn't have to be a people-pleaser all the time. I also learned how to walk away when people hurt me. I could forgive them and speak to them without getting dragged down by the emotional turmoil. I miss Gene terribly. When I'm feeling sad, I hear his voice inside my head that says to pick myself up and put my struggles in God's hands."

Emotions

I was actually looking forward to my doctor's appointment. I was on an emotional roller coaster and didn't know why. I made a point to take good care of myself and knew that something was wrong for me to be so tired. I had never been to this physician before but felt comfortable when she walked in and introduced herself.

"Have you been to a doctor recently, Mrs. Sauter?"

"No, it's been awhile. My previous doctor retired and I put things off the past few years because my husband was ill. It isn't like me to have mood swings and no energy."

After examining my throat and the area around the lower part of my neck, she said, "I knew what was wrong when you gave me your symptoms. Your thyroid is out of whack. I can hear the rattling sounds. You need to address this right away. Please get this prescription filled. You'll need to take the medication about an hour before you eat breakfast. You'll soon notice a change. If you don't, I'll change the dosage."

In no time, I felt like myself again, even though my girls remained concerned about me. For that reason, I wasn't surprised to get a supportive letter from Cindy.

June 4, 2007
Dear Mom,

I know you are going through a lot and trying to figure out your place in life right now. I think of Gene every day. It has been almost a year since you contacted hospice. I know it's hard to be alone and I think it's all catching up with you now. You know he wouldn't want you to dwell on the past but to live life. You're doing much better but try to enjoy each moment.

I know it might have seemed insensitive when I didn't take the kids to visit his grave site. Frank and I thought they were too young for that. They both attended the funeral and we thought that was enough. We believe that Gene is with us in spirit.

Smile, Mom, for you are blessed. You were loved by one of the kindest people on earth.

Love,
Cindy

I printed out the email and put it in the trunk with Gene's other souvenirs. Yes, I was better but I missed him so much. He was my sunshine on gloomy days. I could never forget his smile and endearing words.

Birthdays

My excitement about the trip to Ireland was overshadowed by concern for Mom. When my cell phone rang one afternoon, I was nervous when I saw it was Dad.

"Annie, your mother fell and broke her hip. We were going to see the doctor. I told her to let me help her but she didn't listen. Her hand slipped off the door handle and down she went. She's a mess."

Even though she had wonderful health care workers and therapists who aided in her rehabilitation, she never fully recovered. The fall compounded her other health problems and it became more difficult for her to get around.

She was sitting at the kitchen table one evening while I finished the dinner dishes. We were making small talk when she said, "You know it was George Bush's birthday at the end of June. I sent him a card and a check."

I was glad that my back was to her, so that she couldn't see the hurt in my eyes. I quietly said, "How nice of you."

I couldn't help but wonder where my birthday greeting was when I came to the farm to help her. I didn't expect a gift. I just wanted her to acknowledge my birthday. Why was it so difficult? Why did she seem so distant? I wondered if it was because of her health or something else.

The Sign

Dad was in distress when he called several days later. Mom had quickly regressed to the point that they moved her bed downstairs. Crystal arrived at the farm shortly after I did and by late afternoon, we all knew she needed to be in the hospital.

"Grandpa, I think you need to admit her. I know she doesn't want to go but she's having too much trouble breathing."

When I nodded in agreement, he called 911. Because no rooms were available, I stayed with her in the ER all night. I kept her warm with blankets but didn't hover because she didn't like coddling. When she slept, I prayed that the Lord would watch over her.

As the orderlies prepared to move her the next day, one of them said, "We're taking your mother a different way. Please go to the guest elevators to find her room."

"Thank you. I'll see you in a few minutes, Mom."

When I found the hall to her room, I saw the palliative care sign. I knew it meant that she was at the end of her life but I couldn't get a definitive answer from the staff. Some in the family thought she'd be home soon but I didn't. When I walked in, her nurse was hooking up various tubes. I thought she seemed a little better and wondered if it was because she was out of the ER and finally in her room. A few days later, we were all surprised when her medical team recommended putting her in a nursing home.

She accepted the news better than I expected. After she was transported and settled in, I went to see her. Dad was sitting by her bed. They both looked at me when he said, "Please go on your trip to Ireland. It's okay."

Mom echoed his sentiments.

"Yes, please go, Annie. I'll be back home soon. Do not cancel your trip. You need to get away and take time to heal from Gene's death."

"Now that I see how much better you look, I don't have as many qualms about leaving. I love you, Mom."

"I love you too."

I walked out of her room with a heavy heart, unsure of my decision to honor their wishes. As it turned out, I had a wonderful time exploring the beauty of Ireland with my friend, Dianne. On our last day, we were looking forward to seeing the Cliffs of Moher. I was sitting one seat behind the bus driver when he got everyone's attention and said, "It looks like I have a call coming in."

I froze. My stomach dipped and I said, "It will be for me."

"How do you know, Miss?" the driver said.

"My mother is ill. I almost canceled the trip but my parents insisted that I come."

A few minutes later, he said, "I have a call for Annie."

I trembled as I reached for the phone.

"Hello."

"Mom, it's Suzy. I'm sorry to have to tell you this but Grandma passed away this morning."

I didn't respond.

"Mom, are you there?"

"Yes, honey. I thought it would happen while I was gone. We're heading home tomorrow and I'll call you when I reach Newark. Thank you. I love you."

It was time to say another goodbye and watch another chapter in my life close.

217

Peace

When I returned home from the airport, I dropped my bag, took another from the garage, packed for the funeral and headed to the farm the next day. The wake, which was planned for the 21st, was also my one-year wedding anniversary since Gene's death. I had dreaded it for a long time, having no idea that it would also be the day that I grieved for Mom's passing.

She died peacefully in her sleep. The last person to see her was my brother. I knew she would have wanted to be alone when she drew her last breath.

I was at Dad's by 8 o'clock. After a big hug, he said, "Annie, I can't believe she's gone. I didn't think she would die so soon."

When he started wandering from room to room, I said, "I'm so sorry for your loss, Dad. Are you okay?"

"Yes, I'm just getting ready for the funeral."

After I cleaned up the kitchen, I waited for him in the living room. He was holding a box and Mom's purse when he returned.

"Please find a place to hide these. There are pieces of jewelry in the box. I don't want anything to disappear. You hear about break-ins while people attend funerals. I know your mother has other pieces but I don't know where they are."

"No problem, Dad. I'll find a place upstairs. I'll put her purse on the top closet shelf behind her shoes. I'll take a look around and check all of the boxes and drawers for more jewelry. I know she put some pieces in teacups on top of the buffet. I'll put everything in her wooden jewelry box and will slide it under her clothes at the back of the closet. While I'm doing that, you can get ready. Have you picked out what you're going to wear?"

"No. I need help."

He opened his side of the closet and slowly moved his hands across the clothes. When he tried on his suit jacket, we were dismayed that moths had damaged it. I called my brother immediately.

"You need to take Dad shopping. He has a problem with his suit."

The funeral home arrangements were a patriotic display of Mom's love for America. She would have liked it. During the service, I sat in the front row with Dad and my girls. I stared at the woman in the casket who persevered through so much in her lifetime. I sighed and started to cry. I didn't know if my tears were for Mom or Gene. He had respected her so much.

That evening after everyone was gone, Dad walked into the kitchen while I finished loading the dishwasher.

"Annie, I want you to come upstairs with me. Where did you put your mother's jewelry?"

"Don't you remember? We put it in the closet yesterday behind all the clothes."

"Yes, yes, now I remember. Please get it out."

I pulled out the box and purse and handed them to him. He sat on the edge of the bed and took his time looking at things. Then he held up Mom's sapphire and diamond ring. It was the one from her mother that she always wore.

"What should we do about this ring? I know it's supposed to go to the oldest daughter. That's what your mother wanted. It seems fitting since you were born in France and are the oldest."

I was so touched. I never thought the ring would go to me. When I put it on, I finally felt like I belonged.

Suffering

The day before Thanksgiving, I returned to the farm. Dad had an appointment with the ophthalmologist who recommended cataract surgery in the near future. He was doing paperwork when I arrived. His baggy sweater hung from his shoulders. He looked lost.

When I hugged him, he tearfully said, "It's so rough without her. We shared so much."

"I know you did, Dad. You had many wonderful years together."

His eyes brimmed with tears again as he shook his head in despair.

"I have trouble seeing her clothes in the closet. I should give them away but it's so hard."

I helped him with his jacket. "I'll take care of it when we get home."

We stopped for lunch after the appointment. He spent most of the time telling war stories. As we were pulling out of the parking lot, he said something, though, that I'd never heard before.

"You know, Annie, we all suffered from PTSD when we came home after the war. I wish I had understood at the time."

I wanted him to tell me more but that's where it ended. I wondered if he ever realized how his PTSD affected our whole family. We suffered from it too.

He was worn out when we got back to the farm and was ready to get in his recliner for a nap.

"Dad, I'm going to grab some large trash bags and start working on Mom's closets while you rest."

"Thank you, Annie. I don't know what I'd do without you."

It was so overpowering to see her favorite clothes and those she couldn't part with. I needed a system and decided to put them in piles, according to sizes that ranged from 8-16.

By 3 o'clock, I was drained and by no means finished. It was a more daunting task than I anticipated. Before stopping for the day and taking a relaxing shower, I went into my old bedroom. It could have waited another day but for some reason, I wanted to know right then what was in each letter.

After moving sheets and blankets out of the way, I slowly pulled the heavy box towards me and set it on the bed. I opened the musty flaps and stared at tattered letters scattered among the photos. I had wanted to read them all my life and here they were. Once I put them in order, they dared me to open them. I wasn't sure if I was ready to discover the truth … whatever that might be.

The Letters

Italy
January 14, 1945
Dear Folks,

Day before yesterday, I had some pictures taken. I'm looking pretty good and feel better all the time since getting out of the hospital. I'm still in the redistribution center and will probably remain here for a few weeks. It's nice compared to front line duty.

I know you want details of some of my experiences, so I will share this. In early fall, we made a big move farther up to the Gothic line. We advanced about a mile and went into an old farmhouse. The rear half had collapsed under artillery fire. German infantry had been in earlier that morning. They had run wires up the trail and set booby traps. A misstep could mean death.

One day, a light machine gun section was working on their foxholes when one of our leaders said, "I think there are riflemen ahead of us towards the German lines. Across the draw, about 100 yards ahead is the entrance to an old wine cellar. Let's head over."

Just as we got near it, a barrage of mortar shells came in. That's when I was hit in the lower back by what seemed like a flying stone. It knocked me to my knees and I felt dazed. Captain Sugars was okay but our runner and radio operator were injured. We crawled to the entrance of the winery. Nothing else was left of the structure. We made radio contact about our situation and the following day, a medic came and tended to those of us who were wounded. In the meantime, the Germans shelled the area around us. The next evening, Company F attacked and took the high ground.

I was in a lot of pain and my lungs felt full of fluid when I was put on a stretcher. When I felt my shirt pocket, my Bible was still there. I carried it with me all through Europe. When I arrived at the station hospital, I received sulfa and another tetanus shot. The sight before me was terrifying. There was blood all around and many men were on stretchers waiting for evacuation to hospitals. Some were wounded beyond recognition.

I thought I was on my way to Florence but instead, I was taken to an airstrip nearby. I passed out when I was loaded onto a C-47. I remember the plane gaining altitude before I fell asleep. I woke up on an operating table at the 64th General Hospital in Leghorn. Following surgery on my back, two American nurses in the recovery room said that I repeated wanting to go home.

Then the day came to remove the bandages from my back. As the nurse peeled back the adhesive, it began to take off the skin. The doctor said, "You will have a natural belt scar around your waist for several years. You also have three cracked ribs and double pneumonia."

I was disappointed when the medical staff recommended that I not go back to the 34th division. I was reclassified to non-combat duty and was to return to state-side duty. While I was healing in the hospital, I got bored and helped the hospital staff respond to the patients' needs. I questioned why I survived when many of my friends were blown to pieces. I knew God had a plan for me.

When I returned to good health, I was sent to work at the replacement depot in Naples. At that point, my orders were in constant *turmoil. I was first told that I'd be flying home. That changed when it appeared I would go to France. This was confirmed by a superior officer who said, "Sergeant, you have administrative experience and will assume responsibility for a rear echelon position, while those you replace will see front-line service."*

I suppose you are sitting on the edges of your chairs when news of the campaign comes over the radio. I hope it's the beginning of the end. That remains to be seen.

I hope you are in good health and that things with the farm are going well.

Lots of love,
Charles

Germany
April 17, 1945
My dear Marguerite,

Leaving you last Sunday morning was comparable to leaving home for me. I kept remembering how wonderful it was to meet you and your sister. We had such a good time together. I'll never forget the day I walked into the cafe. You were working in the kitchen and your mother pushed you forward and said, "Marguerite, I want you to meet the nice American." You were so beautiful that my heart stopped.

You will be impatient with me for not corresponding in French. That will come later. Writing in English gives me some vocabulary and if you can read my writing with the aid of a dictionary, it will be more comprehensive.

It is lonesome here after all the social life back there. No fraternization is allowed and I'm glad. I have no sympathy for these people.

Remember our agreement. I promise to return. I will be thinking of you always.

> *Love,*
> *Charlie*

Germany
April 26, 1945
Dear Folks,

I am quite negligent in my correspondence to you. However, when you do not hear from me for a few days, don't worry because my position in relation to the front is not what it was before. All I must be careful of in this country is a few civilians and I don't fear them.

It may sound hard to believe but I met a girl over in France who I care for more than anyone I've ever met. It's hard to describe how much war can affect our lives. Certainly, it has many disastrous effects but it can also give one a new set of codes for measuring what we should value in life.

Don't think I am going to disgrace the good family name but I may have a pleasant surprise for you in the next few years when I return home.

> *Love,*
> *Charles*

Germany
June 3, 1945
My dearest Marguerite,

I am in the office taking phone calls. It has been a nice day and this evening the shadows are long. It reminds me of those nights when we used to take walks along the river. How I wish I could be with you now.

I don't know when I'll be able to see you. It is so hard being apart because the moment we met, I knew that I wanted to spend the rest of my life with you. Of course, as soon as our approval for marriage gets back, I will be sure to see you. My present status will probably change soon. I will let you know as soon as it happens. When I hear from my company in Italy, I will have enough points for discharge from the Army, so we did not put our papers in any too soon. If everything turns out right, we will be married shortly before it's my turn to go home. I am going to request occupational duty, so that I can go back with you rather than returning to the States and later sending for you.

Marguerite, where would you like to go on our honeymoon? If I can get a long pass, how about Paris? We should be able to spend 3 or 4 days there. Darling, it's impossible for me to explain in words the love I have for you.

With love always and thousands of kisses,
Charlie

Germany
June 19, 1945
My darling,

Please do not worry about my parents disapproving of you. It's to be expected that they were somewhat surprised at first when they learned about you. But they have always respected my judgment and want me to be happy. I know you will like them very much and they you. Everything will be fine.

I hope to return to college and finish my studies after we get home. Of course, I won't if you don't like this idea. We would get a house near enough for me to walk to classes. You could also attend school if you wish.

A few days ago, I learned that the usual period of waiting two months before being granted permission to marry was rescinded. In other words, our marriage application papers may be back before August. This is wonderful news!

I long to kiss those pretty lips of yours.
Love always,
Charlie

Germany
July 4, 1945
My darling,

I received two letters from you today that made me very happy. I will soon be leaving my present organization. The new Company will be a supervision center where I will be in charge of issuing supplies and food to prisoners of war.

I am terribly sorry you didn't get a letter from me in such a long time. Do not worry. I will not leave for America without you. Without a doubt, if I stay in the Army, I will be in Europe for six months, perhaps more. If I take my discharge and work for the American Government, I will have to stay here for one year. It would be best for me to stay. Then we could be sure of getting transportation back to America together.

Our application for marriage has been approved by headquarters! We can be married after August 1st. So let me know soon when you'd like it to be. I hope your engagement and wedding rings arrive shortly from home. I want to come soon to see you to make final plans and to talk with the chaplain who will marry us. I want to press you close to my heart.

Remember me to your mother, grandfather, and sisters.

All my love,

Charlie

France

July 13, 1945

My darling,

I've been thinking about you constantly and how wonderful it was to be with you again, even if it was only for a few hours. I'm sorry I kept you awake so long Sunday night. When we're together, it seems like I just can't let you go. I am sending some snapshots of you, Renee and your family. I am keeping three pictures of you. They are exceptional. I am sending one complete set to my parents.

I will get a pass for 10 days when we are married on September 26th. The only thing which could interrupt our plans would be orders for me to report to the United Nations Relief and Rehabilitation Administration in Paris. I doubt if that will happen because it will take a long time for the paperwork to be finished.

There will be many changes for you, Guite, but I am sure you will get along very well. Your happiness and the success of our marriage will be my responsibility. I will teach you the new customs of my country. They will not be very difficult but you will feel lonely at first. Thank you for having faith in me.

Love always,

Charlie

France
October 11, 1945
Dear Folks,

We couldn't have had a nicer wedding. We were married at 11 a.m. at the Protestant Reformed Church in Nancy, France. The ceremony was performed in both English and French. Quite a number of my Army buddies and Marguerite's relatives were there. The wedding dinner lasted for five hours with all its courses. I am so happy being married to my beautiful bride.

I will soon be a civilian and not a sergeant. My new job will give me an officer's privileges but I do not have to answer to Army restrictions in return. My pay will be between what captains and majors make. I'll wear an officer's uniform but with a U.S. insignia only and a discharge patch on my chest.

This next year should be very valuable to me in gaining experience and I intend to make the most of it. I don't care to spend another year over here, but I want to bring Marguerite with me when I go back. Our marriage would have two strikes against it from the start if I would come home and have her follow a year later. I hope to save enough to go back to college in the fall of 1946 or by January of 1947. My current job will be helpful with future employment at home or possibly here if I wish. Many American enterprises are springing up and some like General Motors, DuPont and Standard Oil are making enticing offers now. My best bet would be to go back and finish my education. My work here has shown me what I need to do to be successful. College will have a definite purpose for me now, whereas before I wasn't sure. I don't plan to enroll with any major in mind but will catch up on subjects that are the basic tools I'll need to construct a career.

I shall always be interested in the farm and intend to come back to it but during my work here, I have discovered that I have potential

*for something else and am more proficient in it. I shall probably go
into that type of work.*

I hope all of you are well.
Lots of love,
Charles

Germany
December 11, 1945
My dearest Guite,

    *Today I received your card with the picture of a baby on the
front. Darling, I don't know what to say. I am almost speechless and
when I looked at the writing on the card, my knees had a funny feeling and I had to sit down. It will be wonderful if we have a baby!
Are you sure of it yet? Be careful and take care of yourself. My parents
will be very happy for us but they will be afraid you are not getting
good medical care. Let me know when you want me to tell them our
exciting news. Please write more to let me know how you are.*

Goodnight, my sweetheart.
Love you forever,
Charlie

France
December 16, 1945
Darling,

    *I am very glad today because I received your letter of December
11th yesterday. I know you are very much surprised about the news of
the baby but it's love, love, love!*

It's been a long time since I've seen you. I wanted you here for Christmas but there was no Charlie. Write often because I am very sad when I don't hear from you. In your last letter you said you would come in two weeks. I count the days. I will always love you.

Guite

Germany
December 26, 1945
My darling,

I am very sad that I could not be with you on Christmas. I felt <u>terrible!</u> Most of all, I felt bad because you have just given me the wonderful news that you are going to have a baby!

I couldn't come because there are only 13 of us here to make some kind of Christmas for 7,000 people whose houses have been bombed or cannot return home for political reasons.

I hope we will be in America next year. At Christmas, there will be three of us. I will not tell them about the baby until you say I can.

All my love,
Charlie

Germany
May 8, 1946
Hello darling,

I wish I could explain to you the wonderful feeling I had when I saw you lying there on the bed with our baby daughter. I was very glad to find you looking so good and to know that you and the baby are doing well. I was afraid that something happened to make you have the baby so early. I am so glad you had no great trouble having her. Even though she is very little, she is delicate and nicely made and I'm sure she will grow up to be a very pretty lady like her mother.

All my love to you both forever,
Charlie

France
August 3, 1946
Hello darling,

I received your 2 letters today. One from June 26 and July 3. I am very sad to know you are ill but I think it is not a serious disease. Here all people say your baby is very nice. Annie is a beautiful girl now. She always smiles.

I am very lonely without you. I write to you with Annie in my arms. You don't know how disappointed I am. I wait for you Saturday July 20 all night and Sunday all morning – please tell me why you don't come.

My mother makes a good meal for you and my darling does not arrive. Charlie, you know the time is very long for me. When will you come back for me? People keep asking me where my husband is. I wonder the same thing!

Is it possible for you to come for the marriage of cousin Odette in September? If you don't come, I don't go. I think you should come see your baby before the 27th.

It is impossible for me to stay far from you. Please come get me because some days I feel so lonely.

Love,
Guite and Annie

Germany
November 13, 1946
Hello darling,

    I had a difficult trip back to Wiesbaden as my carburetor continually caused trouble. It seems that there was a lot of dirt in the reservoir and it came up in the motor. It is okay now.

    I showed the pictures of you and Annie to my friends here and they say the baby looks like you and I agree. I was so happy to have 2 days with you again. It is always very hard for me to leave you. Perhaps it doesn't seem that way but it is. With my job, I have no choice.

    We are to move to Frankfurt in 2 weeks and as soon as we have finished the work of organizing our new area offices, I will go on leave.

                        Love,
                        Charlie

France
December 31, 1946
My darling,

    Tonight is the 31st of December, the last day of 1946 and tomorrow a new year begins. I hope it will be a happy one for you and we will always be together. I wish this because I love you and can't be away from you.

    I am alone in my bed tonight. My sister goes to the dance with her friend. They ask me to go but I refuse because I am too sad. My bed is cold without you. I told you I have patience for four months and not more. Pardon me if I am jealous but I love you very much.

            Happy New Year. I give you a big kiss.
                      Love forever,
                        Guite

Germany
January 29, 1946
My darling Guite,

It seems the mail situation is getting very bad. I have had no letters from you but I am sure you have written. Tonight I am on duty at the office until 10:30 p.m. I will have to walk back to the hotel because it was necessary for our garage to be turned back to the Germans.

We are having difficulty getting enough gasoline to operate all our autos and trucks now. There has been so much black market that it is necessary for the Army to diminish the amount given to each unit, so none of the surplus is sold. I was sorry to hear Charles de Gaulle resigned. I hope France can regain some economic stability.

It has been just two weeks since I saw you last but it seems much longer. In a few months, we can always be together. I thank God for the opportunities and events that led to my meeting you. The war was a terrible thing but out of all the bad, there must be some good and that was you.

All the love in my heart to the loveliest wife in the world.

Charlie

France
January 15, 1947
Hello my darling,

Monday I am going with my sister to Strasbourg. I hope you can come very soon with your passport to tell them who you are. The office is open every day and the people in the consulate are very nice. I am going for my passport for America today.

I know you are lonesome but I am too. Please tell me when you *think you should finish with UNRRA. I hope it is as soon as possible because I have had a poor life without you. I know it's the same thing for you.*

Guite

Ohio
February 4, 1947
Dear Son,

We received the darling picture of Annie from Marguerite. We wish you could get a picture of her smiling. She seems like such a sober little soul.

In regards to the money — we inquired at the bank about the best way to send it and they said by New York Bank draft. This will be sent within a few days, as will your two suitcases if they pass mail measurements. I expect to polish my leather hand grip for baby things and will send a suitcase for Marguerite. I think it best to use what we have now and when prices go down, you can buy some nice luggage.

I hope you keep well and have good warm clothing. I worry about you as much by day as I do by night.

Love,
Mother

Germany
April 29, 1947
My darling wife,

Tomorrow is the birthday of our little Anne Marie. I shall never forget that day as long as I live. Please forgive me for not coming on my leave but I have had too much work here. I have a little surprise for you – it is certain that my work will be finished in June and perhaps I will come before then. I am going to try to leave here on the 1ˢᵗ of June if they will let me. Anyway, I am sure I am leaving.

If possible, I would like for you to come here and visit for 2 weeks. Bring Annie if you wish. I have put the papers in but they are not finished yet. Please tell me how long you wish to stay in France after I'm finished with work. I would like to go back in July at the latest.

Guite, it just seems fantastic to think of going home with you and Annie. I shall be as much a stranger as you. I feel like a displaced person myself after so long a time over here. Kiss Annie for me.

All my love forever,
Charlie

Germany
May 18, 1947
Darling wife,

I am packing my things tonight. According to the present plans, I will be coming on the 26ᵗʰ. It's possible they will keep me until the 15ᵗʰ of June because there is much work and no one to do it now.

Your things that mother sent have arrived. It seems we'll have to wait a long, long time for a boat to the States. It may be September before we can go, unless we fly. Perhaps it would be a good idea to do that as far as Annie is concerned. If we have to wait on a ship, we can take our time saying goodbye to everyone.

All my love to you and Annie, sweetheart.
Charlie

Germany
May 28, 1947
My darling Marguerite,

I will come to Nancy on Monday night, the 2ⁿᵈ of June or per-haps Tuesday the 3ʳᵈ. I want you to go to Paris with me so we can get all our arrangements made for going to the States. If necessary, we will go through Holland to get out of Europe.

Do you have your exit permit yet? We have a lot to do to get out and must get everything arranged as soon as possible. Then we will go back to Nancy and wait.

I send you all my love.
Charlie

The letters opened my eyes to what Mom and Dad went through to be together. They loved each other deeply and in a night of passion, I was conceived before their marriage. Mom's emotions were so fragile then. Maybe that's why she didn't want to show me where I was born. She didn't want to talk about those pieces of her past that she had buried long ago.

At a young age, the war forced her to become an adult. She protected her mother and siblings, worked tirelessly at the cafe, took care of me, and left her loved ones behind when she came to America. She must have been miserably homesick for her family and terribly bored at the farm where there was little for her to do. And yet, she made the best of it.

If Dad hadn't been under so much pressure from his family to return home, he might have stayed in France and found employment that he liked and was well suited to do. He and Mom might have been happier if he had been given the freedom to make his own decisions about his future and ours as a family.

The Clothes

We celebrated Thanksgiving at the farm just two short months after Mom's death. I found solace in having everyone together. So did Dad. It was soothing to hear laughter in the house again. After dinner, I asked anyone who was interested to go through Mom's clothes. They were as surprised as I was that she never got rid of anything.

After all the goodbyes and everyone had gone, Dad fell asleep in his recliner for the night. This gave me the opportunity to finish the closet. I knew it would be too hard on him to see her things strewn throughout the room. So I worked late into the night and filled 24 large bags that I stuffed in my car and trunk. I left her favorite red heels that she hadn't worn in years, her pretty pink raincoat and a gray sweater she loved to wear on cold winter days. It was important for him to have a piece of her clothing that he could hold and press against his body.

After lunch the next day, I said, "Dad, it's time for me to leave. I might not be back for a couple of weeks."

"Annie, I always enjoy your company. Thank you for helping me with your mother's things."

He waved from the window when I pulled out and like I had done for many years, I beeped the horn when I got to the road. I made it to the distribution center just as they were about to close. I rolled down my window and said to a personable young man, "Please let me give you these things."

"Sure. Let me help you."

"Thank you so much. Please be careful. These are my mom's. She passed away."

That's all I could say before my lips started to quiver.

After helping me unload everything, he set the bags on top of the others in the large room and said, "Is there anything else I can do?"

"Thank you. You've been very kind."

While I was glad to have that responsibility behind me, my relief turned to sorrow by the time I got home.

Adjusting

My way of coping with Gene and Mom's deaths was to travel every chance I got. I was only home long enough to pay bills, attend a new church, and visit with family and friends. Being alone in the farmhouse added to Dad's grief, so I took him on several trips too. In the winter, we went to Florida. When we left my house and drove to the airport, I wasn't surprised when he said, "Why didn't we drive? It's so much easier."

"Dad, we'll be there in two hours this way."

He used his cane to get around and didn't want assistance from anyone when we landed. When he voiced his impatience at the long line of people at the car rental area, I noticed the automated machines at the side. I told him to hold our spot and I'd be right back. I kept on walking and acted like I didn't hear him when he said, "Don't use that machine. It will only cause problems."

After punching in my registration information, I pulled out the receipt and yelled, "We're ready to go, Dad. Follow me."

As he moved out of the line, he said, "Are you sure you have your paperwork?"

I let him rattle on as we headed out the door and across the parking lot to pick up our mid-size rental that was just like the one I drove at home. Once inside, I plugged in my GPS and entered the address for the resort that I had booked in Orlando. Within seconds, he said, "Do you have a map? I have one."

"Just relax, Dad. We're ready to go."

We hadn't driven far the next morning when we saw a large sign advertising the Ringling Brothers Museum.

I looked at him and said, "Do you want to go?"

"Yes. I've never been there."

We both enjoyed it but didn't leave until 4 o'clock because of his ongoing commentaries at every exhibit. By the time we returned to the resort, I was far more exhausted than he was. I wanted to be with him but it was frustrating that he made me feel like a child.

As soon as our plane touched down in Ohio, he thanked me for a great time and wondered where the next trip would be.

Truth

I looked forward to driving him to Pittsburgh for the 34th Division Red Bull Army Reunion. There had been a good turn-out when I went to the celebration in 1996 but I knew that wouldn't be the case now. There weren't many name tags on the table.

As we walked around looking at the memorabilia, I heard a fellow say, "Ten thousand WW II veterans die every year."

That was a sobering thought. I looked at the man's name tag and introduced ourselves.

"My dad and I are curious how many will be here this year."

"We expect 48 guests."

When Dad started asking about men he knew, we learned that they were either ill or had died. Dad looked at me and said, "We didn't attend while your mother was ill and now so many are gone."

I slipped my arm into his and said, "Let's find our table."

When we returned to the hotel that evening, he talked incessantly about the war. After letting him go on and on, I blurted out the question that I was always afraid to ask.

"Dad, is it true that I was conceived before you were married?"

He sat very still and looked away. He wasn't sure what to say.

"Well, yes. Your mother and I were celebrating Victory Day. We were happy, in love and planned to be married soon. It just happened. I didn't know she was pregnant until December and you were born in April. I was a bit shocked when I got the news. We always felt it was better left unsaid. You were so tiny that we told everyone you were premature. You know how people talk. We didn't want anyone to make fun of you. It was a different time back then. My mother and others didn't accept such behavior."

"Thank you for telling me the truth."

"Annie, I'm sorry I was so hard on you while you were growing up. You know, I was trained to make people obey. It just spilled over into my life after the war. You were a good kid. I'm proud of you. Despite the obstacles, you've worked hard and succeeded."

I pushed back the tears.

"You have no idea what this means to me, Dad."

The Artist

Part of planning a family trip to France in September of 2008 was informing my brother of our plans.

"I'm going to be traveling with my girls and Aunt Colette. She's going to stay with her sister while the girls and I explore France. I had the pleasure of being with Mom and Dad in 1990, so now it's your turn to experience things through Dad's eyes."

Cindy booked our rooms at the Hilton overlooking the Eiffel Tower, which was going to be my first stop. I was anxious about going all the way to the top. The first time I went to France, I was afraid to do it and wasn't going to let my fear stop me again. Once I made it to the first platform, I continued. When I stepped into the open air to look down on the city, I shouted, "I did it!" and asked someone to take my photo. I couldn't help but think of the picture of Mom and Dad standing on the platform so many years before and how bittersweet it had to be for her.

Over the course of the next several days, we traveled to Nancy, spent time with Mom's relatives, visited battlefields, and toured a majestic church that my grandfather helped renovate. When I had a chance to slip away on my own, I walked up to the altar and bowed my head. *Mom, I miss you so much. I forgive you for all that was left unsaid through the years. I understand why now. You worried what people would say. You weren't ready to be a mother. I'm at peace knowing the truth. Dear Lord, I roll her over to you.*

We stayed in Marseille long enough to say we had been there. It had been Dad's first stop on his way north. From there, we traveled to Monaco and Cannes and spent the night in Nice. Earlier in the evening, we strolled down the cobblestone streets and looked at the vendors' art pieces. We were especially drawn to an older gentleman's work. While browsing through his collection, we talked with him at length. After finally saying goodbye, we walked in silence until I looked at the girls and said, "You know who he reminded me of?"

Suzy and Cindy nodded when Crystal said, "We do, Mom. He reminded us of Gene."

"Let's go back, girls."

The artist was happy to see us again and we were all delighted with the paintings we bought that would always be reminders of such an enchanting experience. He rolled and wrapped each painting with care. I was struck by his eyes that sparkled like Gene's. As I reached out to take my painting from his hand, he looked at me and said, "Goodbye, Annie."

How did he know my name? It was never mentioned and we paid in cash. I knew it meant that Gene was saying goodbye.

For the first time since his death, I felt alive again.

On the Go

My life was busier than ever in late March with Crystal's engagement and Suzy's pregnancy. I visited Cindy as often as possible and spent time with friends. I rarely turned down the opportunity to go anywhere and was looking forward to our monthly card party at Bert and Carol's.

Bert greeted me at the door that night and said, "Hey, Annie, it's good to see you. Since our kitchen upstairs is being remodeled, John is down in the mother-in-law suite helping with dinner."

I was surprised that he shared John's whereabouts with me. I glanced towards the stairs when I heard him talking to Carol. They were carrying dishes of food. When he set one on the table, I was struck by his pleasant demeanor and handsome features.

Once we were all seated, I was happy to be across from him. He smiled and said, "Hi, I'm John."

"Hello, I'm Annie."

I reached over and shook his hand.

He engaged in conversation with everyone. I enjoyed listening to him so much that I was sorry to see the evening end. Driving home, I couldn't get him out of my mind and wondered what his reaction would be if I asked him to accompany me to Crystal's wedding. What if he declined? If he accepted, would I call him my escort or companion? It definitely wouldn't be a date.

I woke up earlier than usual the following morning. John was still on my mind and I decided to send Bert an email. I questioned if it was appropriate but I really didn't want to go alone. Hoping that I didn't sound like a fool, I somehow got up the nerve to send it. *Bert, what do you think if I ask John to be my companion at the wedding? If I ask YOU to ask him and he says no, he has said no to you and not me. I haven't been on a date in a long time. This is a scary thing.*

I was so surprised by his quick response that I spilled coffee on my bathrobe. I slowly opened the message that read: *I will ask.*

After returning home from a weekly canasta game several days later, the phone rang. It was Bert.

"Annie, I'm sorry I didn't get back to you sooner but I've been busy at work and couldn't get hold of John. I finally caught up with him today. He said he would be honored to be your companion at your daughter's wedding."

I was silent.

"Annie, are you there?"

"Yes, yes, I'm just surprised. I wasn't expecting a positive reply."

"I'll get back to you later this week. We have an event I'd like you to attend. John plans to go with us. We'll talk soon."

After hanging up, I told myself repeatedly, "This is not a date. This is not a date."

I was nervous all week until the doorbell rang and I saw John's charming smile. After spending a wonderful evening with him that passed much too quickly, I invited everyone in for a cup of coffee. I tried not to make too much eye contact with him but it was difficult. As they started to leave, I hugged Bert and Carol and then looked at John.

"I guess I'll hug you too."

"I hope so," he said with a grin.

I blamed my sleepless night on the coffee but it seemed like much more. A kind, funny and good-looking man had just entered my life.

Small Talk

In the weeks ahead, I appreciated Bert and Carol's invitations to go places, knowing that it would mean seeing John. One of the outings I enjoyed most was visiting a vineyard. It was a gorgeous day and he was so attentive when I described my joy of being in the delivery room when my granddaughter, Gina, was born. He smiled warmly when I explained that Suzy had named her after Gene.

When we weren't together, I looked forward to being in touch through emails.

May 31, 10:58 p.m.
John,

I hope you're able to attend the rehearsal on August 7th. It starts at 5 o'clock and dinner is at Lockkeepers.

Annie

———————————————————————

June 1, 10:52 p.m.
Annie,

I will be available on the 7th. I went for my tux fitting last week. They found one that fit. How would you feel about a practice run for your daughter's wedding? A "friend" and I were invited to a wedding in July. Most of my friends are guys and most don't clean up very well. Those that do aren't good dancers! Therefore, since I assume that I may consider you a friend, I'd like you to be my guest on July 11th if you aren't busy. The venue might be a cross between Mardi Gras and the parole board hearing. This should be a lovely affair. Let me know, so I have time to hold dancing auditions among my other friends.

John

June 2, 3:47 p.m.
John,

Thank you for the invitation. I am free that weekend and a practice run sounds like a good idea. Should I wear a mask and a costume? It looks like a lively evening. I hope I clean up better than the guys!

So glad they found a tux that fits. If you don't mind, I need your address, as I will be sending out invitations soon.

Annie

June 2, 9:41 p.m.
Annie,

A mask and a costume are unnecessary. However, you might consider it if you value your reputation! Only kidding! Just being seen with me is enough to get you on a couple of lists. I am sure you clean up better than the guys. I suspect this will be a first-class event. Most of my mail gets sent to a P.O. Box in Zurich. However, if you send it to my other address, chances are I will receive the letter. Also, the chances are that you might have a visit by a couple of big guys in dark suits with curly wire things sticking out of their ears. They are usually polite and only ask a few questions! Just one suggestion. I like to dance and if you have dress pumps with steel toes, it might be a good idea to wear them.

John

June 16, 8:46 p.m.
Annie,

Here is something to consider. There will be a "beer dinner" at my son's bar on Tuesday, June 23rd. It will consist of six courses of food, accompanied by 5 oz. of beer. The beers will be different for each course and intended to complement that particular food. Bert, Carol, two of their neighbors and more will attend. They said you would not have to drive home afterwards, as they would prepare the guest suite. If this is something you think you would enjoy, join in. Please let me know as soon as possible. I received Crystal's wedding invitation today.

John

June 17, 11:18 a.m.
John,

Hmm, since I have trouble with one glass of wine…what do you suggest? I guess I can do lots of sipping.

Annie

June 18, 8:41 a.m.
Annie,

    Fear not, you will have the assistance of some of the better beer drinkers in town. You can rely on plenty of help.

    If you are here by 6:15, that is fine. I'll have time to give you a tour of the estate, view the cars up on blocks, etc., and get to the bar at a fashionable time. Bert probably has the least flexible time schedule, weekends notwithstanding, but we can figure something out.

John

I wasn't sure how things would go. I hadn't been alone with a man in a long time. I arrived early at his lovely home and enjoyed the tastefully landscaped yard. There with tiers of flower beds that flowed from the house to the driveway and down to the sidewalk. It was obvious that so much detail had gone into planning it.

I had to ring the doorbell more than once before he appeared by the side of the house.

"Oh, I'm sorry I didn't hear you, Annie. No one ever uses the front door. Come around to the side."

A car parked in the drive made for a narrow passageway and as we walked, I bumped into him when he stopped. I excused myself and backed away. He wanted to show me the backyard, so we continued past the door. It was small but very intimate with a pretty patio, freshly laid sod, and flowers and plants everywhere. His two black Labradors fought for my attention as we stood by the fence. While I petted them, I felt like I couldn't breathe. I needed to relax but couldn't.

I was relieved when he said, "Come inside. I'll show you around."

He and his wife had done a wonderful job of decorating the home that was filled with antiques, works of art that he crafted, and paintings by his son. When he started to climb the steps to the second floor, I didn't know what to think. The walls were lined with pictures of his family and he took the time to tell me who they were. It was surreal when I saw his wedding photo. I felt like an intruder.

On the way to his son's gastropub, we exchanged small talk about our lives, until he pulled into the space reserved for "Dad." We had arrived early and sat at the bar, while he spoke to several people who walked by.

He leaned over and said, "Annie, it's okay to relax."

His words put me at ease, as we were escorted to the patio where the meals were served. He made me feel special when I was introduced to his friends. I also appreciated what a gracious host his son had been. It was truly an unforgettable evening.

Once we returned to his house, he invited me in for a cup of tea.

"Thank you, John, but I know you have plans tomorrow."

As I started to leave, the space between us grew smaller. When I brushed past his face, he kissed me on the cheek. I thought about it the entire way home.

John,

I'm finally at my computer and want to thank you for the most outstanding Tuesday evening. I can't tell you when I enjoyed myself so much. It is now ranked in the "top ten" most memorable times of my life. Everything was perfect! Chris is very friendly. I wanted to tell him how great everything was but didn't have a chance.

Your home is lovely. It is filled with character but then a "character" lives there. The work you've done on your back patio is amazing. I couldn't stop looking at the front flower beds when I stood on your porch. Everything was so beautiful.

Enjoy the day.
Fondly,
Annie

Annie,

Glad you had a good time. I did too. We can have tea another time.

What are you doing on July 3rd? I'll be attending a concert at Blossom with friends. Would you like to join us?

John

He was right on time when he picked me up for the outdoor concert. Once we spread our blankets on the ground, we sat close to each other and barely moved the entire night. When he took me home, I received a light kiss on the lips. I enjoyed being with him so much and couldn't wait for the wedding on the 11th.

My Girl

I spent hours deciding what to wear to the wedding. Once I picked out a dress and the bolero jacket that complemented it, I couldn't make up my mind which shoes to wear. I didn't know how my feet would survive the day in the clear plastic heels, so I threw a few more in my bag.

When I turned down John's street, I noticed several cars parked in his drive. I couldn't imagine who was visiting when he had somewhere to go. I walked to the side door and knocked several times. I could hear laughter, so I pulled open the screen door and shouted, "Hello!"

John quickly appeared in the kitchen. He greeted me with a kiss, took my hands and said, "I love that dress! Let me introduce you to my kids who just dropped in."

With his hand lightly touching my back, he walked me to the family room where I met his two sons, their wives and his grandchildren. His younger son said, "Hey, I've been hearing a lot about you. It's nice to finally meet."

I sat down and talked to everyone until it was time to go. We left the house but soon found ourselves back in the drive as John had forgotten the gift and his jacket. Once we were on the freeway, we laughed about the timing of his family stopping by. When we arrived at the church, he walked around to open my door and extended his arm.

"I'm old-fashioned, Annie."

I slipped my arm through his and said, "I love old-fashioned."

He held my hand throughout the ceremony. When the time came to share the peace with others, he kissed me on the lips. After we arrived at the banquet hall, we sat on the patio with our drinks until it was time for dinner. I didn't know if it was the drink or just John's company. He looked so nice in his blue jacket that I had trouble keeping my eyes off of him. I couldn't help myself. All kinds of thoughts ran through my head for someone who had been labeled "prim and proper" all her life.

Following the delicious meal, the band started to play. He held me close and guided me across the dance floor, whispering "my girl" as the song continued. When we started gathering our things to leave, another slow song started to play. He pulled me back on the dance floor and held me close once more.

We talked about the wedding until we got back to his house. I was completely relaxed when he said, "Would you like to come in?"

"Yes, but just for a little bit because you have to be up early tomorrow."

When he came over to my side and opened the door, my dress moved up when I swung my leg around, exposing my thigh. I heard him sigh. He told me to make myself comfortable in the family room and asked if I'd like a cup of tea. I knew the caffeine would keep me awake most of the night.

"No, thank you. Just some water."

When he sat down beside me, we held hands and talked about trivial things. When my nerves started getting the best of me, I said, "It's time for me to go. I had a wonderful time this evening."

I stopped at the landing in front of the side door and when I turned to say goodnight, he took me in his arms and kissed me passionately. When I eventually pulled away, he said, "You have to leave just as things are getting interesting?"

"Yes, I really need to go."

As I backed out of his drive, I waved and said, "Have a good time in Nashville!"

During my 25-mile drive home, all I could think about was that kiss. I was pleased to see his email the next morning.

Sunday
July 12
Annie,

I had a great time. We met some characters and the company was friendly. You looked super. That was a lovely dress. I'm just getting ready to go fishing.

Talk to you later.
John

Alarm

I left for Buffalo on Wednesday to visit Cindy and her family. I knew I needed a diversion to keep from thinking about him constantly, so I played some of my favorite music on the way. As the week progressed, I was disappointed that I didn't hear from him. I knew he was busy working but I had hoped he could find some time to be in touch. In a moment of self-doubt, I said aloud, "This dating stuff is such a game at our age. You never know where you stand."

When I returned home, I went straight to the computer to check my emails but there was nothing from him. I reminded myself that he would not be back again until the 23rd. Before falling asleep that night, I prayed for his safety.

The next morning, I jumped out of bed at 6:30 and walked around the block. The day was off to a good start until Crystal called to share a dilemma.

"Mom, the Independence Home Days are the same day as my wedding. It's no wonder that date was available. The parade is at noon and the wedding is at 1 o'clock. This is going to cause all kinds of parking issues."

Once I convinced her that things would work out, she calmed down. When we finished talking, I sat down on the sofa to relax. A few minutes later, the phone rang again. Much to my surprise, it was Carol. Since John was out of town, I couldn't imagine why she was calling.

"Annie, this is Carol."

"Hi. It's good to hear from you."

My heart sank when she said, "Are you sitting down?"

"Yes, I am. What's wrong?"

"John is okay but he had a stroke last night. He was eating at a restaurant. Luckily, a nurse was nearby. They were able to get him to the hospital in time and administer the necessary medication. He's in critical condition."

I felt like I was going to pass out.

"We were on a date last weekend, Carol. That's the last time I saw him. He kept forgetting things. Maybe that was a sign."

"Both of his sons have flown down. I want to give you one of their phone numbers."

I jotted it down and repeated it back to her.

"Thanks for letting me know, Carol. I really appreciate it."

I paced back and forth, not knowing what to do. After stressing out for nearly an hour, I dialed the number. A tired voice answered.

"Hello. This is Annie. We met last weekend at your dad's house. I'm so sorry about what's happened to him and I apologize for bothering you but I have to know more."

"Don't apologize. I'm glad you called. When we arrived at the hospital, Dad was paralyzed but the drug reversed the effects. It was like a miracle. We watched him get better in front of our eyes."

"Thank you for sharing this. Is it okay if I call him?"

"Yes, let me give you the phone number. He may have trouble speaking, so be prepared."

I carefully dialed the number. His voice was shaky when he answered.

"John, it's Annie. I want to tell you I care. I'll call again tomorrow."

Every word was slurred when he said, "I'm glad you called. Thank you."

His speech improved with each phone call that followed. I never spoke long … just long enough to send best wishes.

"John, I hope you won't get tired of me when you get home but I will visit often."

"I won't, Annie. I promise."

Days later, he said, "I have some good news. My sons will be driving me home from Nashville on Friday."

A shiver ran down my back, as I thought of the long drive and the toll it would take on him. I worried that he was being discharged too soon.

Carol called on Friday morning and said, "I wanted to let you know that John and his sons got home at 2:30 in the morning. They're all sleeping in. John has a doctor's appointment today and he knows that I'm going to take him."

"I'll make their dinner tonight, Carol."

After hanging up, I debated what to fix. Lasagna was always a good choice, so I made a list and went to the grocery store. I arrived at John's, just as his son was parking his car by the curb. While he helped me carry the food to the kitchen, he filled me in on his dad's progress. When we walked in, John and Carol were talking. I was amazed how good he looked. He seemed a little tired but he was talkative and able to get around. I welcomed his heartwarming hug.

As I put things on the counter, Carol said, "The doctor's visit went well. He has to give himself injections until he's ready for the Coumadin. Thank you for fixing dinner tonight."

"It was my pleasure. I've made plenty of food. Please stay."

"Thank you for the invitation but I need to go home. It's been a busy day."

John's other son, their wives and grandchildren soon arrived. They talked at the table while I set everything out for dinner. The lasagna was a big success. Everyone had a delightful time and it was obvious how happy John was to be home. The sound of his laughter gave me goose bumps.

After I finished cleaning up the kitchen, they all encouraged me to join them in the family room. When I sat down, I said, "I hope you don't mind but I'd like to stay here tonight and sleep on the sofa. I know you're all tired and I could be an extra body in the house."

The guys nodded their heads in appreciation and thanked me for my concern.

After everyone left, John put his arm around me and we watched TV the rest of the evening. I knew he had to be tired but when I mentioned it, he said, "I'm not ready to retire for the night."

Just before midnight, he rested his head on my shoulder. I gently nudged him and said, "You'll be more comfortable in your bed."

He didn't argue and let me help him climb the stairs. After everything he'd been through, his agility and balance were surprisingly good. Once he was in bed, I headed for the sofa where I tossed and turned all night.

The sound of the dogs whining woke me up early the next morning. I was surprised that John didn't hear them. At 7 o'clock, I stood at the landing and loudly said, "The dogs are calling you. I'd let them out but I'm afraid they'll get aggressive."

When there was no answer, I said, "John, the dogs are whining."

I began to feel anxious when I went up to check on him. His door was open and I could see him in bed. He was on his left side. I called out again but there was no answer. Fear surged through me until he slowly started to move. I breathed in relief when he said, "Oh, I guess I overslept."

"That's fine. You needed the sleep."

He greeted me with a kiss and said, "Good morning. Sorry I slept so long. I'm going to get the dogs. Make yourself comfortable."

I had planned to make breakfast until I realized there was no milk or juice. When he came back, I said, "There isn't much in the refrigerator. Let's go out for breakfast."

"Okay. That's a good idea."

I went into the bathroom to do something with my hair. I hadn't brought any other clothes, so I had to go as I was. John stood outside the door and said, "My wallet is in the bedroom. I'll be right back."

I watched as he carefully maneuvered down the stairs. When he reached the third step from the bottom, he grabbed his stomach and said, "I don't think my medicine agrees with me."

I put my arm around his waist and helped him to the sofa where he collapsed. When his left arm dropped to his side, I grabbed my phone, dialed 911 and frantically said, "I think John has had another stroke! He had one a week ago. Please hurry!"

More Alarm

The lady who answered calmly said, "Who are you and what is your relationship to the patient? What is the address?"

I all but yelled, "Please, can't you ask these questions when you get here?"

"I'm sorry but I need some information. What is the address?"

"Give me a second. I have to look at the front door."

I stumbled back into the house and told her, followed by another plea to hurry. As soon as I hung up, I called Carol. My body was shaking when I said, "I think John has had another stroke!"

"Oh, no! Did you call 911?"

"Yes. I'm going now to tell his son!"

I stepped out the front door but wasn't sure which way to go. Then I remembered seeing the kids run to the left the night before. I could hear sirens in the distance and ducked back into the house to cover him up with a blanket.

"Please stay where you are, John. I have to tell Chris what's happened but I'm not sure where he lives."

He tried to point but he couldn't move his arm or speak. I raced outside, turned to the left, and ran through the flower beds until I reached what I hoped was Chris's porch. I rang the doorbell several times. The sirens were growing louder when he opened the door. I was out of breath and stammered, "I-I had to call the EMS. I think your dad's had another stroke! Hurry!"

"I'll be right over!"

After the technicians examined him and carefully placed him on the gurney, they asked Chris questions about the first stroke. When we got to the hospital, we chatted nervously in the waiting room until the doctor came out.

We were numb when he said, "Your father has had a second stroke. He may have to learn to feed himself, talk and walk again. We don't know at this moment."

When we were allowed to see him, I concentrated on his face and not the tubes and wires attached to his body. I touched his hand gently and whispered in his ear, "I will see you through this. I love you."

The Message

The rain fell softly on Crystal's wedding day that was filled with breathtaking moments. Even though John wasn't with me, I smiled throughout the ceremony and maintained my composure. After her father and I walked her down the aisle, I took my seat and purposely kept a space to my right … a place to remember two men who couldn't be there.

I couldn't help but think of my wedding day to the girls' father years ago. I wanted so much more for them on their special day and I did everything possible to make it happen. My heart overflowed with love when Crystal and Joe stood at the altar. As Gene's stepson, Don, approached the podium, I took a deep breath. He was holding a sealed letter that Gene had written to Crystal…a token of his love that he wanted shared on her wedding day.

Before reading it, Don said, "I met Crystal when she was five years old. Although a generation separates us, we are united by one special relationship. We shared a stepfather in Gene. He lost his first dear wife to cancer in 1964 and raised their four children. He later married my mother. My brother and I were already grown at that point but Gene put some of the finishing touches on my life as a young adult. He and Annie married in 1987. They had a wonderful marriage and once again, he had a hand in raising Cynthia, Suzy and Crystal. The ring that Joe will be wearing on his left hand is the same wedding ring Gene wore when he married Annie.

Before Gene passed away in November of 2006, he composed this letter. I am privileged to be able to read this to you."

June 20, 2006
Dear Crystal,

I hope this is the happiest day for you and Joe. May you have the happiness that your mother and I had. May you enjoy life as we have. I know you will.

Please don't try to save the world because it can't be done. Live one day at a time and make each one count.

Be kind to your mom.
Love you much,
Dad

It was such a sincere blessing. I continued to smile through the mounting tears that wanted to fall. Joe took the handkerchief from Crystal's hand and wiped his eyes, while she brushed away her delicate tears. After Don finished, he took the empty seat beside me, kissed my cheek and whispered, "I'll walk you back up the aisle."

I was in a fog at the reception and never felt like I was present in the moment. My feet seemed to stay in one place. The crowd of people overwhelmed me and thoughts of Gene took over. I wanted to stay near those who knew me well and our love story.

I thought a lot about John too. I wanted to call him but was afraid he'd feel bad that he couldn't be there with me. I pictured how handsome he would have looked on the dance floor. After the reception, I looked forward to returning to my room. I needed to be alone with my emotions.

A warm shower felt good the next morning. I packed my things and took the elevator to the first floor. When the valet brought my car around and helped me put my bags in the trunk, I said, "I need to get my daughter. I'll leave the car here for a moment."

I called Cindy and she quickly joined me in the lobby. We were off to get Crystal's car, take it back to the hotel, pick them up and whisk them off to the airport. After saying bon voyage, we went back to the hotel for breakfast with Gene's family. From there, we drove to Suzy's. After the whirlwind subsided, I planned to go see John.

Recovery

He spent several weeks in the hospital. I went nearly every day in the late afternoon and usually stayed until 10 o'clock each night. In the beginning, I sat by his side and held his hand but as he improved and learned how to navigate with a walker, we took short strolls in the halls. Because of his determination, he made great strides with his rehabilitation and finally reached a point where he was ready to be discharged. Carol and Bert kindly offered to be his caregivers in their home until his recovery was complete.

I had lunch ready when they pulled in. I went outside and watched, as they helped him out of the car. He looked weak. I smiled with encouragement and said, "Would you like to eat?"

"I'd like to take a shower first. It's been too long."

Bert's son helped him and when he returned to the kitchen, he said with slightly slurred speech, "That felt wonderful. I'm ready to eat now."

Even though I had things cut up to make it easy for him to assemble a sandwich, he struggled. Once he'd eaten part of it, he said, "Annie, thank you for lunch but I'm tired. I want to sit on the sofa."

Bert's son helped him get comfortable and within a few minutes, he was asleep. After I cleaned up the kitchen, I told Carol that I'd be back the next morning.

"You don't need to come that early, Annie. If you would make sandwiches for lunch again, I'd appreciate it. John loves peanut butter and jelly. They told us at the hospital that he needs to feel independent and should do things on his own as much as possible. I need to run some errands right now. Could you please stay a little longer?"

"Absolutely. I can stay all evening."

By 8:30, he was ready for bed. I patted his arm and said, "I'm going home now. Would you like me to come back tomorrow?"

"Yes, please come back."

In the weeks ahead, I spent a great deal of time with him and was overjoyed when his balance, speech, sight, and left arm mobility improved. Although he still struggled with dizziness, we were all amazed by his progress. I wanted to cry when I saw him walk without assistance for the first time.

One afternoon, he repeated a comment that he'd made in the hospital.

"What you see is what you get, Annie. I'm not much good to anyone."

"Let me be the judge of that, John."

Care

The last time I visited Dad, he said, "Why don't you move in here with me, Annie?"

I was torn. I knew he was lonely but I also knew that I could never live with him. He would never treat me like a capable adult. I continued to visit often and stayed in touch.

As difficult as it was, I began to pull away and not see John as much. He needed his space to feel independent and whole again. Because many of his days were busy with visiting nurses and rehabilitation, I started arriving later. Whenever it was time to leave, I always said, "Do you want me to visit tomorrow?"

His answer never changed.

"Yes, I look forward to seeing you."

By the end of the summer, his mobility had improved dramatically. He used a walking stick and sometimes held it up to show off. The need for two people in the house at all times had come to an end. I marveled at his resolve to take back his life. I had a flashback to that day in the hospital when one of his family members said, "Annie, most women would have run but you stayed."

"I could never turn my back on him. I stayed because I care."

Maybe

After spending several days in Buffalo, I looked forward to the drive home and seeing John. When I turned on the radio, one of my favorite songs was playing. The lyrics were a reminder that I could give him a love that would last forever. We hadn't been in touch while I was gone, which gave me a lot of time to think and pray. I felt like our relationship was in God's hands. I would wait for him to decide what he wanted to do with his life and whether or not he wanted me to be part of it.

I called him the next day to let him know I was home. He said, "Come over now and tell me all about your trip."

He met me at the door with a kiss.

"John, you look tired. I don't have to stay."

"I am tired. It was a long day of therapy. Watch TV with me."

He took my hand when we sat down and I shivered when his other hand rested on my leg. I knew he didn't want me to leave.

"I wish I could go back home, Annie. It looks like it will be several more weeks until the kitchen is renovated. I should be moved in by early December. That's when I'm planning on going back to work. I appreciate all that Bert and Carol have done for me but I want to get on with my life."

I marveled at his inner strength. He refused to give up. After he returned home and went back to work, we saw less of each other. I missed him and began to second-guess the trip I'd planned months earlier. It was hard to imagine being at Marco Island for five weeks in late January without him. Even though we talked frequently on the phone while I was gone, it wasn't the same. When I returned home in March, he let his feelings be known.

"Annie, I like you very much. I never thought I'd be in a relationship with anyone else after my wife, but I want to know you better. Will you move in with me?"

I felt sure of myself when I said, "Yes, I'll move in. Let's give it a try. I think it will be important for us to keep some of our routines. I'll go back to my house twice a week to play cards with my friends, pick up the mail and pay bills."

"I agree. I don't want you to give up anything. After work every day, I'll continue to exercise and stay in touch with my close friends. On weekends, we'll ride our bicycles, go to art shows and visit family and friends."

"I look forward to all of it, John. I really do."

When we were doing the dishes one evening, he said, "What if we take a trip south? I want to show you New Orleans and introduce you to great food. We can take our time. I have vacation left. We can head to Charleston and Savannah and then go on to Mobile. I'll do some of the driving but I'm not sure I can do it all."

"That sounds like fun. I can help with the driving. I'm just thankful that we're even talking about traveling after everything that's happened."

Our last night in New Orleans was enchanting. While standing on the balcony, he embraced me and said, "I wasn't looking for someone but I have fallen in love with you so much."

Little White Chapel

One evening in July, we were at his son's restaurant when John reached into his jacket pocket, pulled out a small box and laid it in my hand.

"I'm tired of calling you Mrs. Sauter. I want to call you Mrs. Lieb."

Caught by surprise, I said, "Do you realize that last year at this time, we had our first date? We were at the wedding."

He kissed me and watched as I slowly unwrapped the gold paper. Inside the black box was a solitaire diamond ring.

"John, it's beautiful!"

"I hope this means you'll marry me."

"Yes, I'll marry you! I love you."

After a lingering kiss, he said, "I hope we can have at least 10 years together."

I didn't have a response. Why did he say only 10 years? I looked forward to being together much longer than that.

We began making wedding plans right away. I couldn't go along with a traditional wedding, out of respect for our deceased spouses, so we decided to elope. I was excited when he said, "A lady at work told me that she and her husband got married in Vegas and had a great time. Elvis walked her down the aisle. What do you think?"

"I think Vegas sounds great. Let's do it."

"I know a fellow out there who can be our witness. I'll call him tomorrow. I'll email the person in charge of scheduling weddings and see what we have to do ahead of time. Let's shoot for January."

Before I knew it, we were flying to Vegas to be married at the Little White Chapel where Elvis walked me down the aisle. We had so much fun and never regretted our decision for a second. When we returned home, we discussed what furniture he wanted to move to my house. I encouraged him to bring pieces that would make him feel comfortable. Because he was still unsteady on his feet, I removed all the rugs. He had to be careful that he didn't trip. He was on a blood thinner and one fall could result in serious consequences.

We did things together whenever possible. He joined my Friday afternoon card group and I went to the shooting range with him on Wednesday mornings. I appreciated so many things about him, including his support of time spent with my grandchildren. When our children invited us over, we gladly went but made a conscious effort not to interfere in their lives.

Goodbyes

I was on my way out the door when John said, "The doctor just called. The blood test results are back. There's an iodine buildup in my thyroid. He wants me to see an endocrinologist tomorrow who's going to run a radioactive test. That will help them know how to treat my condition."

"Okay. Do you want me to go with you?"

"Yes. That would be nice."

I kissed him goodbye and said, "This is just a quick trip to check on Dad. I'll be back in plenty of time for your appointment."

I arrived at the farm at 8:30 and was surprised that Dad hadn't unlocked the door. It was unusual for him to sleep that long. When I peeked into the bedroom, he was snoring away. After making a pot of coffee, I checked my emails. By then, he walked into the kitchen.

"Oh, Annie, thank you for coming. I hope you haven't been waiting long."

"No, I just got here a little bit ago. What would you like to eat?"

"Just two sunny-side up eggs, bacon, toast and coffee. That's all."

He was noticeably quiet when I fixed his breakfast. He only told one story. When he finished eating, he wanted to go for a ride. He was so unsteady that I took him by the arm and helped him into the car.

"Where do you want to go, Dad?"

He pointed to the left but then changed his mind and said, "No, that isn't the way. We have to go right."

He made several more mistakes, which was concerning. So was the fact that he didn't reminisce about anything. After we got back to the house, my younger brother walked in and said, "Hey, are you both ready to watch the game? Ohio State plays in a couple of minutes."

Dad didn't answer, so I said, "We're ready."

After helping him to his chair, we were soon jumping up and down, giving him a high-five each time the Buckeyes scored. When he barely reacted, it was even more obvious that he wasn't himself.

I pulled away from the house with a heavy heart the next morning and called my brother.

"I left early because John has a doctor's appointment. Dad is probably still asleep. Please check on him today if you have a chance. Something is going on."

"Yep, no problem."

I was up early the next morning and was making a pot of coffee when the phone rang.

"Annie, I found Dad on the floor beside the bed this morning. I was checking on him before I went to work. He hit his head and was disoriented. I called an ambulance."

"Do you want me to come now or is this just to alert me?"

"It's just to alert you."

An hour later, I received another call.

"They're taking Dad to Riverside in Columbus. He has a bleed on the brain."

"We'll be there as soon as we can. John should be home any minute."

When we arrived, Dad had been moved to the neurointensive care unit. By late afternoon, his eyes were closed and he was no longer alert. At 6 o'clock, the doctor came into the room and said, "Due to your father's other health issues and his age, we don't recommend further treatment."

We gathered around him. In honoring his wish, we knew that we had to let him go. There was comfort in knowing that he wasn't in pain.

The next day, I couldn't join my siblings and Crystal at the hospital. John was scheduled for a second thyroid scan and I wanted to be there. When we returned home, he went to the rec center and I fell asleep on the sofa, which was something I never did. When I woke up, I felt a surge of energy and prayed out loud. *Dad, I forgive you. I understand things now. It was your PTSD. I know you loved me in your own way. I loved you too. Please let go and be with Mom. She's waiting for you. Dear Jesus, I roll him over to you to take him home.*

When I raised my head, I looked at the clock. It was 3:55. A feeling of lightness came over me. It was peaceful.

A few minutes later, the phone rang. It was my brother.

"Annie, Dad passed."

The next day, I called my sister-in-law who was holding Dad's hand when he died.

"I'm so thankful you were there. Do you remember what time it was when he took his final breath?"

"I think it was around 3:55. He squeezed my hand and was gone."

When I told her what happened the previous day, we both cried. I was deluged with emotions and said, "He was with us."

When John arrived home, he held me in his arms until my last tear fell. I had finally connected with my dad.

Healing

Shortly after Dad's death, John received a phone call from his doctor. I cringed when he said, "They have to change my medications, Annie. I'm going on prednisone."

"It's a dangerous drug. My friend swears that's what caused all her health problems. This worries me, John. It could be the start of trouble."

Because we were driving long distances to some of his appointments, it was a relief when he found a new internist who was closer to our home. Upon reviewing his records at our first visit, the doctor said, "Due to your health conditions, you shouldn't travel in the coming weeks."

We followed his orders and canceled our New Year's Eve Caribbean cruise and our month-long stay in Florida. We didn't travel anywhere while the doctor tried to regulate his thyroid. In February, he saw an orthopedic surgeon for fluid on his right elbow and was diagnosed with bursitis and bone chips. We were told to use ointments and a wrap.

A few weeks later, he called me while I was having lunch with friends. I was surprised to hear from him because I knew he was at the shooting range with his buddies.

"Hon, one of the guys noticed that there is seeping through my elbow wrap. I called the doctor and he wants me to go to the hospital as soon as possible."

I could hear the anxiety in his voice.

"John, I'll be there right away."

Following surgery, a lab report indicated a bacterial infection. A PICC line was inserted in his arm and I administered an antibiotic at home. Six weeks later, the cast was removed and it was obvious that the spot hadn't healed. He underwent another surgery and was discharged the next day. Even though the stitches were left in longer, the six-inch incision was open when the cast was removed. I was appalled when I saw it and had to look away.

The doctor threw his arms up in the air and said, "I don't know what to do. I'll have to refer you to my friend who is a plastic surgeon."

I forced myself to control my temper when we were sitting in the plastic surgeon's waiting room. After the examination, he looked at us with confidence and said, "You will have to take care of the wound with Clorpactin and wrap the elbow three times a day until the wound vac procedure on June 20th."

I looked at the calendar on the wall. It was only May 23rd.

I said, "Well, I guess this is what happens when patients are on prednisone and the doctor doesn't take them off of it before they go into surgery."

The surgeon didn't comment.

We felt better about things a few days later when we learned that he would go off the prednisone and methimazole on June 6th. Our hopes were dashed, though, when the endocrinologist called. John hung his head and said, "Annie, now that I'm off the prednisone, my thyroid is off. They're canceling the wound vac until it's regulated."

I packed the wound and wrapped his arm for three months, three times a day, praying all the while that it was healing. He finally had surgery on August 20th. The doctor took a vein from his wrist and placed it in his elbow to help the blood flow. He took more skin from the stomach and used it on the wrist. After one week, the wound healed.

On a follow-up visit at the hospital, the doctor said, "Yes, the prednisone could have possibly caused the problem."

I looked at him and said, "No, it did cause the problem."

The Travelers

I was delighted that John enjoyed traveling as much as I did. In the spring of 2013, he suggested a cruise to Alaska and an Amtrak trip to Seattle and California.

"What do you think, Annie?"

"I've been to all three but would love to visit them again. The railroad trip sounds like fun. Keep in mind, though, that we're going to France in June. Is that too much?"

"No, I have the money and the doctor says I'm doing well. So let's go."

We had a wonderful time. After everything that he'd been through, it was difficult not to get emotional. I was so thankful that he was able to enjoy everything. When the doctor told him that he was physically able to travel, there was no stopping our wanderlust. When we traveled to Europe, I rented a car and drove him all over France. In addition to visiting my relatives, I also took him to Germany to visit places where Dad had worked after the war and where John's ancestry originated. In the spring of 2015, we went on a cruise on the Danube River and took a bus trip through Scotland and Ireland in the fall.

Not long after we returned home, I noticed him struggling with anxiety one morning.

"John, what's wrong?"

"I just get so overwhelmed at times. There are days when I'm not sure how to handle everything."

"I know this is easy for me to say but put your doubts and worries in God's hands. Turn them over to Him."

"Hon, I watch how you are and I know that's what I should do. I'm trying. I lose my way sometimes but I'm learning."

Periodically, I looked at my wedding ring from Gene. I knew I'd never wear it again but wanted to do something special with it. After giving it a lot of thought, I decided to separate the diamonds and make three rings for the girls. The following week, I described my idea to a jeweler.

"I'd like to use these gold bands and have the diamonds divided equally. Then I'd like to purchase a third band of white gold for the remaining diamonds. Can this be done?"

"Of course. They should be finished before Thanksgiving."

When I picked them up, I marveled at their beauty and envisioned the girls' expressions when they opened their gifts. Shortly before I handed them out, John walked over to the sofa where the three of them were sitting and said, "Thank you for accepting me into your lives. I love you all."

I had no idea that he was going to do that, so I was already in tears when I put the gifts in their hands. After many hugs and kisses, they agreed that the rings were the best gifts I'd ever given them.

Life was good. Many people made a point of telling John how healthy he looked. Although he had moments when his balance was off, he continued to exercise and take good care of himself. I was in awe of his energy and his ability to make the most out of each day. When he learned about a new Viking Ocean Cruise, he said, "Annie, let's sign up. As long as my health holds out, I want to go. It looks like the best way to see eight countries in 15 days."

As it turned out, we were too late for the cheaper fares for 2016, so we booked a trip for late April in 2017. I couldn't think of a more meaningful way to celebrate my birthday.

For several months, he had been working on a gunstock for his grandson. The artistry was incredible. His original plan was to give it to him on his birthday in October but he changed his mind and said, "You know, it will be better if I wait until Christmas. It will mean more. I want to have a special gift for my granddaughter too. I've saved some rubies that could be made into a necklace and earrings. She's old enough to appreciate something like that. I want to make shadow boxes for my sons. Will you go with me to pick them out? They need to be the right size for these old fishing lures and other mementos."

"I'd be happy to help. Just let me know when you're ready."

"I'd like something special for my daughters-in-law too. What should I get?"

"What about starting a charm bracelet for each of them?"

"That's a great idea. You need to pick out charms for yourself too. That is my gift to you."

"John, you've already given me a special gift."

"Really? What's that?"

"Your love."

Catastrophic

After a night of playing bingo with friends, I got home earlier than expected. When I walked in, John yelled, "Hi babe. I'm in here watching the football game."

I threw my coat on the chair and sat down beside him. I noticed that his hand was in a clenched position and asked if it was bothering him.

"Boy, Annie, it's really tight. I've been working on that gun stock ever since you left."

"You might have just overdone it. We've both had busy days. I'm ready for bed."

"I'll be in shortly. I'm tired too."

I fell asleep right away but woke up in the middle of the night when John made a strange sound.

"Sweetheart, are you okay?"

When he didn't respond, I quickly turned on the light. His body was making distorted movements that terrified me.

I called 911 and the lady who answered said, "Can you get something hard under him?"

"What do you mean?" I said desperately.

"Like an ironing board."

"I don't have one like that! Please send someone right away!"

I was afraid that he'd roll onto the floor, so I threw on a bathrobe and stood beside the bed. The EMS squad arrived quickly and transported him to the local hospital. Even though I sensed that this stroke was more catastrophic than his others, I wasn't prepared for the doctor's dire news.

"Mrs. Lieb, your husband has had a massive stroke. Seventy-two percent of the left side of his brain is gone. We want to transfer him to the main campus to operate. He'll be flown by helicopter."

Everything was a blur after that. I never stopped praying while x-rays were being taken. When I heard the doctor's footsteps, I looked up. In a compassionate tone, he said, "We've determined that it's too dangerous to perform surgery."

John's children and my girls and I sat by his side for three days before he opened his eyes. He couldn't talk or swallow. He had a living will and we knew that he didn't want to live life as a vegetable.

In anguish, I said to his doctor, "I don't understand why this happened. He took his medicine, exercised and ate right."

"Mrs. Lieb, studies show that within 4-7 years after a second stroke, the person will have a third one."

I was stunned.

"No one ever told me that. What can we expect?"

"John's brain is severely damaged. He will never be himself. He won't be able to walk or eat and will have tubes everywhere. It will take 4-5 people around the clock to care for him."

Not long after that conversation, he was moved to hospice care. We took turns being with him. I left the house at 4 a.m. to avoid traffic and stayed until 3 p.m. His sons and family came during the late afternoon and took night duty.

We had plans to attend a wedding before his stroke. We were looking forward to it because my granddaughter and grandson were going to be the flower girl and ring bearer. I had decided not to go until family members insisted. They told me repeatedly that I needed a break. I finally consented and wore my black raincoat to conceal the clothes I had worn to the hospital.

When I pulled onto the freeway and drove along the lake, I saw places where John and I had been. I felt like he was beside me. From the moment we met, I was captivated by his zest for life. We were like two teenagers in love.

The next night, I was awakened by a stabbing pain on my side that burned and itched. The inflamed area looked like bite marks. I was fairly certain that I had shingles, even though I'd had the vaccine. I was miserable with the discomfort but didn't have time to go to the doctor. I needed to spend every day with John.

He seemed agitated when I arrived the next morning. When I kissed him, he opened his eyes, raised his hand until it rested under my chin and looked at me with a blank stare. My tears flowed when he dropped his hand and closed his eyes.

I stayed until 1 o'clock. By then, the burning on my side had turned into extreme pain. I kissed him and whispered in his ear, "I played our favorite song on the way to the hospital today. We always felt like the lyrics were written for us. We gave our hearts to one another completely, John. I love you."

I played the CD until I got to Suzy's house. I was thankful that she had taken a vacation day to prepare for the holidays. We were sitting at the kitchen table when my phone rang. It was the hospital.

"Hello," I said in a trembling voice.

"Mrs. Lieb, your husband has passed."

I sobbed at the finality of her six words. When I found the strength to raise my head, I stared out the window. I was reminded that the future's not ours to see but with God by our side, we will never walk alone.

This gives me hope.

Epilogue

We all have a story to tell and this is mine. Growing up, I loved reading about Cinderella. I identified with her feelings of being left out and different from the others. Of course, I always dreamed that I would meet a Prince Charming who would sweep me off my feet and we'd live happily ever after.

At a young age, Meme said, "Annie, if you have faith the size of a mustard seed, He will be by your side." That was ingrained in me. When I listened to my dad practice his solos for weddings, I memorized the words to the Lord's Prayer and "You'll Never Walk Alone." They lifted my spirits when I was lonely.

My journey with Bob was difficult but I walked away with three beautiful daughters. I never looked back. Through it all, I grew stronger in my faith and stronger as a woman.

Yes, Gene was my Prince Charming who came into my life at a very turbulent time. He was the love of my life and meant everything to me. Our lives together were not without challenges but we leaned on our faith and found our way. I miss him every day.

I always felt like I lived my life backwards. John and I were together at a time when we could enjoy simple pleasures and grand trips as a retired couple. He lived life to the fullest and was so young at heart for his age.

I was so shattered by his death that I needed professional counseling to help me cope.

I could no longer run to the farmhouse for refuge. It was sold to a young family after Dad's estate was settled. I was happy to know that the house was alive again. That's how I needed to feel … alive again. Gene and John would have wanted that for me too. So I found pleasure in volunteering for different things and helping my family and friends. I also decided to start traveling again. My friend, Dianne, and I went on the trip that John and I canceled, and I took Aunt Colette to Vegas and the Grand Canyon. I also made several trips to Florida to visit Gene's daughter, Jane. In 2019, my neighbor, Carolyn, invited me to go to Israel with her. I was grateful for the opportunity and looked forward to exploring the places I heard about in the Bible.

When we returned home, I said, "Well, if that is the last trip I ever go on, that was the best!"

Little did I know when I said those words that COVID-19 was lurking like a predator, waiting to shut down the world. Not being able to see family was so hard on me, like it was for everyone else. I made concerted efforts to stay as busy as possible. I continued listening to Joyce Meyer's sermons every morning on TV and immersed myself in Bible study. We met in person on Wednesdays at the home of my friend, Linda, and Zoomed on Thursdays. I also joined two Life Groups led by my friends, Brian and Russell. They, along with others, have been instrumental in my spiritual growth. As I'm writing this, I'm reminded of my late friend, Barb, who went with me on youth group adventures and women of faith outings. We grew together and she will always hold a special place in my heart.

A small group of us in my neighborhood gathered to make over 1500 masks during COVID-19 before they were available in the stores. Along with others, I walked every afternoon, despite the weather, and some of us reached out to neighbors with various acts of kindness. During this period of isolation, I stopped and evaluated my life. I had been involved in so many things. When I realized that I was spreading myself too thin, I devoted myself to focusing on my grandchildren.

I loved my parents immensely. They were both wounded souls who loved their family. They were survivors who persevered, in spite of one hardship after another. Their stories of bravery were admirable. They have inspired me to press on with my faith.

There have been many rewarding experiences in writing this story. I've learned so much. Not long ago, I received an email from Cindy that I'll always hold dear. She described spending time with Dad and hearing a war story that I had never heard. This unforgettable experience is best told through her eyes.

From the time I was a little girl, I spent one week on the farm every summer with my grandparents. I looked forward to Grandfather's stories about WWII in Italy and France. I played with his military medals and when I asked about each one, he would talk for hours. As I grew older, I always made an effort to visit them and hear his same stories. Instead of being bored by the repetition, I told myself to listen and appreciate them, not knowing if it might be the last time I would ever hear them. Grandma always sat at the kitchen table and listened. She never spoke much about the past. In fact, I learned more about her life from Grandfather because she couldn't bring herself to talk about it. So many of her memories were too painful - memories that I didn't fully understand until I went to France when I was 35 years old.

My whole purpose in going was to meet the people and see the places I heard so much about growing up. I met my relatives, saw where Mom was born, where Grandma grew up and where she was married. I was transported back in time when I stood at the train station where the family waved goodbye to Mom and Grandma. I loved seeing the cafe and the park where my grandparents went for walks. This is when I started to realize how hard it was on her to leave France and move to America - to leave her loving family and the beautiful French countryside.

In the summer of 2010, my husband, Frank, and I planned to take our children to Italy. Before we left, we visited Grandfather on Memorial Day weekend. I wanted him to know that we'd be in Italy when the family celebrated his 90th birthday. Without hesitation, he pulled out a photo album I had never seen before. As he began telling stories about the war, he recalled names of people in the pictures and details about the blown-up buildings. He was reliving the scars from his past. In retrospect, I wish I had taken notes or recorded everything he said. I knew this was a gift that we were receiving.

When he turned to one page in particular, he told us that when we visited Florence, we needed to go to the Ponte Vecchio and see the plaque that thanked the American soldiers in the 34th infantry division for saving the bridge - the only bridge the Germans did not bomb in Florence during WWII. Instead, the Germans bombed the buildings on either side of it so that people and trucks could not cross over. Grandfather was involved with special operations (prior to the CIA) and shared that he was part of the negotiating team that prevented the bridge from being destroyed.

When we visited the Ponte Vecchio, we were dismayed that the plaque thanked the Germans for not bombing the bridge. Because it was a covert operation, no one knew the difference. I took a picture of the plaque, as Grandfather instructed, and then took a family picture standing on the bridge that he helped save. I wanted to honor his story and his service. When we returned home, I never told him what the plaque really said. I wanted him to remember it as it should have been.

In 2017, I had an opportunity to travel to Florence. I, too, stood on the Ponte Vecchio. After our guide was finished with her lecture, I spoke with her privately and said, "You know, that story isn't the truth." After I told her the real story, she said, "That's remarkably interesting. I never heard that before. Thank you for sharing."

I will always wonder if my head injury as an infant and the fall-out from my dad's PTSD contributed to my learning struggles. I'll never know for sure but perhaps it contributed to my language and cognition deficits. I do know that my hives were a result of stress and anxiety.

When I was young, I remember students dropping out of school when they had trouble learning. Sadly, many of them were considered less intelligent than their peers and were often made to feel inferior. Instead of applying stigmas, it is important to recognize and embrace the fact that we all learn differently. School systems now have programs to address students' various issues. I wish this had been available for me. While my learning struggles were never specifically addressed or medically diagnosed, I think I had Attention Deficit Hyperactivity Disorder (ADHD). When I taught, I identified with students who preferred hands-on learning activities, had trouble concentrating, were impulsive and sometimes hyperactive.

I am forever grateful for all of my blessings. I will continue to help others and live my life with joy. I believe in God and trust Him to give me peace.

But those who hope in the Lord will renew their strength. They will soar on wings like eagles; they will run and not grow weary, they will walk and not be faint. (Isaiah 40:31 NIV)

Thank you...

I couldn't have completed this book without my editor, Beth Huffman. I met her while walking in my subdivision where she and her husband had recently purchased a property. When she mentioned that she was a retired English teacher who was now a book editor, I shared that I had been writing a story since 2005. When we parted, she said, "Our paths will cross again, Anne."

Fast forward to the fall of 2021 when she posted an update on Facebook of the most recent book she'd edited. When she encouraged people to contact her if they wanted help getting published, I sent her an email that read: *I may need to talk to you.* She responded immediately and said: *I'll be in touch soon.* She called in December and we began the process of compressing and editing my story.

Thank you, Beth, for making my story a reality. I couldn't have done this without you. I had given up on getting published, knowing I lacked the writing skills. God placed you in my life at the right time to complete my journey. You are an amazing woman who walks with courage and never gives up. I admire you and appreciate our friendship.

I also want to thank my publisher, Emily Hitchcock, for paving the way.

I'm thankful for my daughters who have encouraged me to write the book. They were so patient in listening to the endless stories through the years. I am so proud of these strong and caring women. They are wonderful mothers who love and support their children unconditionally.

I am eternally indebted to my loyal friends who have been by my side, regardless of what I was going through. You know who you are. Many people come and go in one's life but it's true friends who stay. Thank you for being my lifelong friends.

Finally, I want to recognize and thank Sergeant Major Justin LeHew, a highly decorated United States Marine who served in the War on Terror. He has been awarded many citations for valor that include the Navy Cross and the Bronze Star with Combat Distinguishing Device denoting Valor. He currently is the Chief Operating Officer for the world's most successful, private MIA search and recovery organization, History Flight.

Justin and his wife took time out of their busy schedules to have a lengthy phone discussion with me. He explained the effects of PTSD on soldiers and listened when I shared what my father went through. He understood when I described how difficult it was for Dad to return home and adjust to civilian life. He answered the questions that had plagued me for years. Justin, thank you for everything you do for veterans and thank you for helping me find closure. You are an inspiration.

CPSIA information can be obtained
at www.ICGtesting.com
Printed in the USA
JSHW011909210223
38052JS00005B/35